Praise for *Bass Pl[ayers to Know]*

"*Bass Players To Know* is a fun and deeply [informative read that manages] to go beyond the obvious mainstream in[formation and teaches you] about some truly unique voices on the bass. By the time you're done, you feel like you really get why these players matter - in large part because of Ryan's carefully crafted 'BPTK' format, consistent throughout the book, which really makes the information stick. Highly recommended!"
—Bryan Beller (The Aristocrats, Joe Satriani, Dethklok)

"This book is wonderful. Ryan Madora struck a perfect balance between providing biographical information on these bass players and providing insight into their musical contributions. There's just enough theory to make it interesting to bass players who understand theory, and not too much to overwhelm those who don't."
—Gerald Veasley (Solo Artist, Educator, Grover Washington, Jr.)

"*Bass Players to Know* is a fantastic addition to the pantheon of bass books in the world. Ryan Madora is both professional bassist and overall purveyor of bass knowledge which is clearly shown with passion in her writing and musicianship. Our industry is altogether better with her in it and *Bass Players to Know* shows us just that!
—Mike Lull (Owner and Luthier, Mike Lull Custom Guitars)

"This book has reinvigorated my interest in the players I'm familiar with and given me a good education on those I hadn't studied before. Great resource!"
—Dave Avenius (CEO, Aguilar Amplification)

Bass Players To Know

Learning From The Greats

By Ryan Madora

Bass Players To Know

Learning From The Greats

Copyright © 2019 by Ryan Madora
All Rights Reserved
ISBN - 9781689573658

Printed in the United States of America
A Division of Mad Ry Music
www.ryanmadora.com
www.bassplayerstoknow.com

Edited by Michael Ross

Cover Art by Leanne Bridie

This book is dedicated to the bass players of the world.

Thank you for everything that you have given the musical community and for what you inspire me to do each day.

Contents

Acknowledgements   i
Introduction   iii
Forward   vii

Section I: The Sound

Willie Dixon	1
Paul Chambers	7
Bob Babbitt	12
Duck Dunn	16
David Hood	20
Tommy Cogbill	25
Leroy Hodges	29
George Porter, Jr.	33

Section II: The Band

Jack Bruce   41
Bill Wyman   46
Rick Danko   50
Tom Hamilton   55
Paul Simonon   59
Cliff Burton   63
Tina Weymouth   68
Krist Novoselic   73
Mike Dirnt   78
Colin Greenwood   83

Section III: The Session Ace

Ray Brown   91
Red Callender   96
Joe Osborn   100
Bernard Edwards   104
Louis Johnson   109
Willie Weeks   114
Michael Rhodes   119
Sean Hurley   124

Section IV: The Eclectic

Richard Davis	131
Bob Daisley	136
Bunny Brunel	141
Richard Bona	145
Tony Garnier	150
Edgar Meyer	154
Gail Ann Dorsey	160
Chris Wood	164
Justin Meldal-Johnsen	169

Index	175
Suggested Listening	183
About The Author	187

Acknowledgements

Quite a bit of time and effort goes into writing a book. This particular one is the culmination of years of listening, writing, researching, and finding needles in haystacks. It's the result of inspiring conversations while waiting to soundcheck, editing columns from the back of a van, and hanging out with other bass players who let their guard down and embrace their inner nerd. And now for some specifics...

Thank you to Michael Ross for your wisdom as an editor and Leanne Bridie for your eye for design.

Thank you to Corey Brown and Kevin Johnson at No Treble for providing the bass community with a fantastic resource for information and for giving me the freedom to write creatively.

Thank you to Craig Haller for being a constant source of support and encouragement, a champion of artistic integrity, and an amazing partner in life.

Thank you to the friends, teachers, mentors, and fellow musicians who help make the musical community a world worthy of being part of. Special shout-outs go to Casey Wasner and Derrek Phillips for inspiring a deadline; to Kyshona Armstrong, Ellen Angelico, Alicia Michilli, and the other powerhouse women in Nashville who remind me to stick to it. Thank you to everyone in the Philadelphia music scene who inspired, supported, hired, and encouraged me from the beginning—Don Evans, Chet Makowski, Greg Wright, and Gerald Veasley.

And thank you to the people who make the gear that allows bass players to be the best that they can be, including the folks at Aguilar Amplification, D'Addario Strings, Mike Lull Custom Guitars, Moody Leather, and Westone.

Introduction

I remember the first time I heard a bass line I wanted to learn. I was at a friend's house, sitting on their living room floor, listening to Nirvana's "Come As You Are." At that moment, I was infatuated. It sounded like something I wanted to possess, to physically hold in my hands, and to have ownership of. I didn't just want to listen to it, I wanted to *play* it. It wasn't long before I got a bass, sat down with the record, and figured it out. Thanks, Krist Novoselic, for helping me discover my true love.

For most instrumentalists, the inspiration to play music comes from hearing a song and wanting to connect with it in a deeper way. We want to feel close to it, understand it, and find satisfaction in playing it for ourselves. We go through phases of listening and digging deep—of spending hours trying to figure out exactly which notes were played and how. Every now and then, we take the time to learn *who* played those notes and maybe give a face to the name. We want, or rather, we *need*, this deeper connection to the music and its creator.

As we mature as players, we owe more and more to the records that continue to inspire us. They are the teachers that we take for granted, the matches that light the fire of our insatiable curiosity. These matches can often be easy to find, as they are sitting next to the record player, given to you by a friend, or mentioned during a lesson. Other times, we pick them up by happenstance while chatting at a restaurant, standing at a concert, or cleaning out the basement. Sometimes they just show up in a drawer somewhere. This book is meant to serve as an entire box full of matches, a lifetime supply. Please, take a minute to strike each one and bask in the brilliance of its light.

Those matches, the records and the players on them, are worthy of study and appreciation. They've given us more than we could ever thank them for. They have given us lessons—and free ones at that—with every listen to every song. The lessons settle deep into our psyche, like a continuously revolving disc of information that forms and informs our musical identity. We should, at the very least, know the names of the teachers we've had.

When I began writing the "Bass Player To Know" series, I pulled from my inner circle of musical inspiration. They were the groove masters, the rock and rollers, the guys from my favorite bands. As the series continued, that list went from five to ten, from ten to one hundred. It forced me to look beyond the players I personally idolized. I began turning to songs that I heard time and time again on the radio, to players whom trusted friends recommended, or to classic albums that thankfully happened to be in my husband's record collection. It has sent me on a never-ending treasure hunt where I discover one piece of gold at a time. Thousands of album credits, countless interviews, and a constant state of inquiry has resulted in plenty of x-marked spots.

As you make your way through this compilation, please understand that this list is by no means complete (it will likely require second, third, and fourth volumes). This book focuses on the players you might not stumble upon as a casual listener or novice to the instrument. It is not meant to diminish or disregard the importance of the "bass greats," because they are absolutely as worthy of deep study as the players highlighted here. Instead, it assumes that you've probably taken time to investigate the Jacos and Jamersons on your own and that you are now inclined to venture beyond the beaten path. My hope is that you are encouraged to revisit the players you have heard of and that you have a desire to sit down and listen to the ones you haven't.

For those of you looking for inspiration, I urge you to read and listen with an open mind. Each of these players have contributed to the development and lineage of the instrument. Some of them have pushed the boundaries of what could be played and how. Others are masterful technicians, creative thinkers, or punks with an attitude and something to prove. They are musical. They are inventive. And some of them, you may not like. Whether you prefer the players who keep it simple and support the song or those who stand in the spotlight with all of the tone and personality they can muster, these are some bass players you should know.

Forward

When I initially developed the concept for the "Bass Player To Know" series of columns for the No Treble site, I made a conscious effort to differentiate between doing a column that was biographical versus one that focused on style. In this day and age, it's relatively easy to stalk people on the Internet, discover who their friends are, where they went to high school, and when they played on their first hit record. Biographical facts are all well and good, but aside from making you feel a bit more informed or proving beneficial in a music trivia game, they aren't necessarily going to improve your bass playing.

What I believe *is* beneficial is the act of critical listening and interpretation. Each piece contains just enough biographical information for you to understand the general arc of an artist's career as well as their greatest achievements and associations. This is followed by a discussion of what I believe is the real reason to know the player: their individual playing style and tone; the musical elements that make their playing unique; and how they have contributed to the evolution of the instrument and recorded music.

To catch each of these artists in the act, I have provided three listening examples that reflect their style. Whether they are classic hits, deep cuts, or excerpts from solo projects, I encourage you to take time to listen to the recordings with an open mind and keen ears. Hopefully you'll like what you hear and will decide to dig a bit deeper on your own. If these listening examples don't exist in your personal library, I encourage you to seek them out.

And now for bit of organization...
As I began thinking about how to format this book, I realized that I had to come up with a method of organization—a way to make sense of dozens of different columns in a way that would best reflect the player, their career, and the impact they've had on the musical community. In other words, I couldn't just create an arbitrary list.

At first, I considered alphabetizing. While this notion made sense on paper, it didn't seem appropriate to have the reader go from learning about one of the greatest power trio players of all time, Jack Bruce, directly to the legendary jazz upright bassist, Paul Chambers. Both are amazing, but not necessarily in the same ballpark. Scratch that idea.

Next, I decided to organize players by genre. Some players are easy to pin down; e.g., the guys that play punk rock usually play a lot of punk rock. Others are a bit more elusive. They're session players who have played on movie soundtracks and R&B records, who have toured with alternative rock artists and produced pop records. They are simply musical people who are chameleon-like in nature. So much for that idea.

And finally, I began to ask myself questions about how the player became a Bass Player To Know. How did their career take shape? What were the decisions they've made, or phone calls they've answered, that determined their place in the world? In addition to being a bass player, how else do we think of them? I realized there might be something to that...

When we think of players, we often categorize them with a simple statement: "So and so from this band" or "an L.A. guy" or "part of The Motown Sound." And then you have the players that excel in so many ways that the best we can do is describe them as eclectic, or less formally, "a badass."

Whether you play bass professionally or as a hobbyist, you continually define your place in the musical community. You begin building a reputation that combines your personality, ability, and the impression you've made on other people. This reputation is what gets you in the door, books you on a Friday night club date, or secures a two-week run on a tour bus. As you learn about each of these Bass Players To Know, you'll realize their reputation is based on the arc of their career and by what people are most likely to whisper about them when they walk into a room.

To make sense of these mysterious whispers, you'll find the book divided into four sections. *In general,* each section chronologically organizes players based upon their overall career style and reputation. There are exceptions to every rule, as most players tend to evolve over time and take part in a variety of musical projects, but most fall into one of the following categories:

The Band: There's a funny saying that goes something like: "You aren't a true fan of the band if you don't know the name of the bass player." Whether you agree or not, for the purposes of this book I believe it's a valid statement. After all, if fellow bass players don't care to learn about each other, who will? The success and overall sound of a band is due to the sum of its individual parts, and the bass players listed here have a lot to do with that.

The Sound: Playing on a hit record is a good way to become a Bass Player To Know. Being the person who played on enough hit records that they defined a new genre is even more impressive. These players forever live on as a notable member of a particular rhythm section—one that created "the sound" of a specific time, place, label, or studio. They are legendary, they are unique, and they set the standard for how to play the instrument.

The Session Ace: When you look at album credit after album credit and continue to see the same handful of names, you can't help but be amazed, slightly baffled, and perhaps a bit jealous. These are the players who can play just about anything with anyone. They've made a career as a first call session musician and have played on hits, flops, demos, top ten records, and everything in between.

The Eclectic Career Musician: Touring, session work, education, production, you name it, they've done it. These are the players who have excelled in multiple arenas, particularly those with a 10,000+ capacity. They've traveled the world, made a bunch of records, and have enjoyed a diverse and eclectic career as a working musician.

For your reading pleasure, feel free to experience this book start to finish, linger on a particular section or bounce around at will. If you're particularly curious about session players, then jump right in, the water is fine. If you'd prefer to read about the players in alphabetical order, then start at Bob Babbitt and enjoy. If this book happens to live in your bathroom and you decide to page through it randomly to satisfy your general curiosity and perhaps inspire your daily listening, then go on with your bad self.

The purpose of this book is to highlight the people who have made the bass what it is today, shed light on why certain records sound the way they do, and help you find inspiration as a bassist and an artist.

Section I:

The Sound

Willie Dixon

It's time for you to play some blues. Perhaps it's in a garage, where you're jamming with friends for the first time and someone suggests playing a "Blues in E." Or maybe during a lesson, your teacher writes out the 12-bar chord progression and plays through a simple box pattern. Possibly, it's on stage at a gig, when the band underestimates the set length and uses an early Rolling Stones or Zeppelin tune to tack on five minutes of playing time. Regardless of why, when, where, or how, if you are playing a blues, the bass line you play can probably be traced back to the efforts of one legendary player, writer, and arranger: Willie Dixon.

Who Is Willie Dixon?

Willie Dixon was born in Vicksburg, Mississippi in 1915, where, through exposure to gospel, blues, and country, he developed an early interest in making music. He moved to Chicago in 1936. There, he split his time between boxing and singing harmony with local groups. Eventually, Dixon had to choose between the two.

Introduced to the bass by fellow boxer and guitarist Leonard Caston, he began playing and recording with the Five Breezes, the Four Jumps of Jive, and the Big Three Trio. While playing around the local blues scene, he ran into Muddy Waters and the Chess Brothers, which led to working as a writer, arranger, and bass player at Aristocrat (soon to be known as Chess) records.

Although Willie Dixon holds his own as a great vocalist, he wasn't typically the featured artist on many Chess records. Instead, he made his mark behind the scenes as a bass player and writer. Muddy Waters, Little Walter, and Howlin' Wolf popularized songs now considered blues standards, such as "My Babe," "Hoochie Coochie Man," "Spoonful," and "Evil"—all written by Dixon. Despite the popularity of his songs and the publishing royalties accrued by Chess and Arc Music (Chess records' publishing affiliate), Dixon didn't see much financial reward or recognition for his contributions.

As the 1960s ushered in the British Invasion, bands like the Rolling Stones, Cream, and Led Zeppelin all took cues from Dixon's music, either by covering his songs outright or by not-so-subtle "inspiration." Various copyright battles ensued, both between Dixon and Arc Music (so that Dixon could regain copyright ownership) and between Arc Music and Led Zeppelin for their use of Dixon's works. When the copyright battles were resolved, Dixon finally found himself credited and compensated for some of his earlier work. Inspired by this turn of events, he spent his later years focusing on his own career as an artist and working as an educator and spokesman of the blues. Dixon died in 1992, having helped to shape the sound of modern post-war blues.

Let's Talk Style
With a deep and well-defined upright tone, Willie Dixon's style is remarkably similar to his stature and personality... stately, solid, and sociable. His bass lines are the hallmark of modern blues playing, since not only did he write most of the songs that we now consider standards, he was one of the first recognizable bass players on the blues recordings that permeated the popular music market. Prior to the efforts of Chess records, most of the early blues recordings either featured solo artists or were of such poor quality that the bass was inaudible.

Many of the blues bass patterns that we learn, from pedaling the root note, to playing the "box," come straight from Dixon's playing. Those patterns emphasize notes from either the major pentatonic scale or the blues scale and are derivative of the left-hand boogie-woogie piano style. Defining much of what we understand as blues harmony, Dixon would often play a minor 3_{rd} in the bass to accompany a major or dominant chord played by the guitar or piano.

In some cases, his bass line can be considered the hook of the song—"Bring It On Home" and "Spoonful" are both built on bass lines that establish the fundamental riff. He also used elements of call and response, a time-honored tradition in blues music, where the instruments state a particular pattern and the vocal line acts as a response.

Rhythmically, his feel was unparalleled and very much in sync with the drummer, the soloist, and the song arrangement. He defined shuffle patterns with keen attention to note duration—some patterns have short, staccato notes, others glide in an effortless, legato fashion. Dixon's experience singing the lower harmony in vocal groups certainly entered into his placement and phrasing, where he created a simple and percussive part in the lower register of the instrument.

Consistency is perhaps the most essential quality of Dixon's bass playing; his dedication to a particular groove and pattern allows for all of the other instruments to fall in with their particular parts. It was typical for him to settle into a bass line and never veer from it, save for a few embellishments at the turnarounds or a chromatic line of passing tones to transition from chord to chord. Dixon also tended to further simplify a part—he often pedaled the root note with greater force to complement the energy of the vocalist or soloist during a particularly dynamic moment.

Where Can I Hear Him?

"Back Door Man" Willie Dixon, *Poet Of The Blues*

With Dixon's growling vocals and powerful lyrics, there's no doubt that this is one of the great blues standards. The song kicks off with a superbly funky, straight-time bass groove that leaves space for the snare accents on the upbeats. Dixon executes the groove consistently throughout the song, with a slight slide into the first root note that mimics a vocal glissando. He leaps up to the octave, emphasizes the minor 3_{rd} of the chord, and returns to the higher octave and $b7_{th}$ to complete the two-bar phrase. Each note is heavily punctuated, clearly defining the time and providing a bounce to the song. Although he adds a few variations during the turnaround chords, the groove provides the perfect and essential pattern to propel the song.

"The Seventh Son" Willie Dixon, *I Am The Blues*

Featuring the famous blues box pattern, this tune is a great example of feel, structure, and stops. The groove, sometimes known as a double shuffle, is characterized by two staccato attacks of each note (the drummer complements the rhythm with two hits on the snare and cymbal). Although the notes are simple (root, 5_{th}, $b7_{th}$, and octave), the staccato execution and steadfast adherence to the pattern make it a particularly powerful feel. Following the piano solo, you'll also hear a break for bass and keys, where Dixon executes a quick, chromatic descending line.

"Rock Me"

Willie Dixon, *Willie Dixon and the Chicago All-Stars*

When it's time to listen to a slow blues, this is a particularly good tune to pick. A commonly requested classic, this includes the "Hoochie Coochie" hook (1-4-b3) on the one chord, a walking line through the other changes, and huge dynamic shifts to complement the intensity of the solos and lyric. Dixon pushes the dynamics of the song by pedaling the root with added force and by including a descending flurry of notes.

Paul Chambers

Name any genre of music and certain bass players immediately come to mind. British Invasion? Paul McCartney. Blues? Willie Dixon. Funk? Larry Graham. They pave the way, define the role of the instrument, and create classic lines that we can't help but listen to, learn, and hope to emulate. They establish the standard with their tone and musical approach—the benchmark to which we often compare ourselves. If you're unfamiliar with Paul Chambers and his contribution to the world of jazz, then transport yourself to New York in the late 1950s and learn about this incomparable bass player to know.

Who is Paul Chambers?
Born in Pittsburgh, Pennsylvania in 1935, Chambers spent most of his adolescence living with his father in Detroit. He originally took up baritone horn, followed by tuba, and finally the upright bass. During high school, he focused on classical music, playing with the school symphony orchestra and various ensembles. Upon

discovering jazz and bebop, he began performing around Detroit and was introduced to jazz guitar legend Kenny Burrell. Chambers took his first touring gig with Paul Quinichette and after completing a tour, decided to move to New York City.

Following a few years of playing in New York with artists such as J.J. Johnson, Benny Green, and Jackie McLean, he was introduced to Miles Davis and joined the trumpet player's quintet. Playing alongside Sonny Rollins, Red Garland, and Philly Joe Jones, Chambers became a mainstay in Davis' band, playing on most of his recordings in the 1950s and early '60s, including *Cookin'*, *Milestones*, and *Kind of Blue*. John Coltrane eventually replaced Rollins in the group, which led to another longstanding musical relationship and the records *Blue Train*, *Soultrane*, and *Giant Steps*, among others. Before his unfortunate death at the age of 33 in 1969, Chambers had recorded with Gil Evans, Lee Morgan, Cannonball Adderley, Wes Montgomery, Wynton Kelly, and released a number of solo records.

Let's Talk Style

Chambers' playing style defined the historic be-bop era of jazz with iconic bass grooves, a sophisticated approach to walking, and knowing how to interact with the other members of the combo. He established the parts on many *Real Book* standards, including "All Blues," "Freddy Freeloader," and "Giant Steps," making him one of the world's most listened-to bassists. As if that weren't enough, he was one of the earliest players to integrate bowing into jazz, a technique that had remained mostly in the classical world.

Chambers' walking lines displayed a deep knowledge of melody, harmony, and voice leading, particularly in how he always seemed to be "one step ahead" by implying the upcoming chord in a progression. He often navigated through changes with the motif of thirds, providing greater harmonic definition to the chord and using the 3_{rd} as a leading tone if moving in fourths. Combining chromatic and whole step motion, he also created melody lines to add variety, rather than simply outlining the arpeggio or playing the root and 5_{th}. This allowed him to land on different chord tones, such as the 2_{nd}, 5_{th}, and 7_{th}, providing a linear approach to the bass lines.

From a rhythmic standpoint, he defined the quarter-note feel of a walking line with the greatest of ease. There was a sense of motion to his playing, making the listener feel like the band is being pushed along with the momentum of each attack. While the drummer plays with rhythmic subdivisions, drives the ride cymbal, and chatters on the snare, Chambers provided the fundamental groove. He added embellishments by executing quick triplet fills, exploring the range of the instrument, and engaging in dialogue with other players.

His ability to support the jazz combo, both rhythmically and harmonically, was the result of listening to the other players and instinctually knowing where to place notes. Chambers created a unique bond with the pianist, often Bill Evans, and the two interacted and responded to one another in a clever and telepathic manner. They created parts, much in the same way a rock and roll rhythm section would, and took turns filling in the gaps and adding colorful variation.

Where Can I Hear Him?
"The Theme"
The Paul Chambers Quartet, *Bass On Top*

A technically challenging and upbeat tune from one of his quartet albums, this highlights Chambers' use of bowing, a technique that had previously been underrepresented in jazz. Kicking off with a catchy, trill-based theme at the head, he jumps into a bowed solo complete with difficult runs and melodic themes. Most of these themes are repeated two to three times, with unique variation to give way to a new phrase. Following the solo, he uses a fingerstyle walking approach to support the other soloists, later returning to the bow as he "trades fours" with the drummer and finishes the tune with the head.

"So What" Miles Davis, *Kind of Blue*

Perhaps one of the most iconic bass lines in jazz, the tune begins with interplay between Chambers and pianist Bill Evans. Evans drops out to give way to Chambers' performance of the main theme, played with confidence and groove, before he settles into a walking line. An ideal study in modal jazz, Chambers plays creatively with one chord rather than directing the band through a series of changes. Throughout the song, he moves effortlessly around the neck, clearly identifying the harmonic background as each soloist is free to improvise. Every now and then, he breaks away from walking and plays with a pattern that favors the root and octave. This adds variety and places greater emphasis on the walking pattern once it returns.

"Four On Six" Wynton Kelly Trio, Wes Montgomery, *Smokin' At The Half Note*

This jazz standard begins with Paul Chambers and Wynton Kelly playing a unison line; a perfect study of root-5_{th} movement. When Wes Montgomery joins the party, the band executes a series of synchronized hits. Throughout the solo sections, Chambers anchors the band with a brisk walking line before embarking on one of his signature bowed solos.

Bob Babbitt

Commonly recognized for his work at Motown's Hitsville Studio A, Bob Babbitt's career as a session player took him to a wide range of places, including the music hubs of New York, Philadelphia and Nashville. His jovial nature, keen understanding of harmony, and unconventionally funky approach made him the perfect addition to the soul records that we all love.

Who Is Bob Babbitt?

Although the "Motown Sound" is greatly associated with James Jamerson, Bob Babbitt was another a staple bass player on the Detroit R&B scene. During the late 1960s and early '70s, Babbitt frequently recorded at Golden World Studios, a competitor of Motown at the time, with artists such as Edwin Starr and The Capitols. This led to touring with Stevie Wonder, with whom he recorded "We Can Work It Out" and "Signed, Sealed, Delivered." These records were made at Motown's studios, where Babbitt was quickly able to establish himself as an in-demand session player. He ultimately contributed to Motown hits by The Temptations, Gladys Knight, Marvin Gaye, and many others.

After making his mark on the Detroit session scene, Babbitt relocated to New York and frequently commuted to the City of Brotherly Love. Working with producers Gamble and Huff at Philadelphia International, he laid down the bass on a number of Philly Soul hits. Babbitt eventually made his way to Nashville, a city that still had a thriving session scene. In the 2000s, he began touring with the remaining Funk Brothers following the release of the movie, *Standing in the Shadows of Motown.* Unfortunately, the music world lost Bob Babbitt on July 16th, 2012 at the age of 74.

Let's Talk Style

You'd be hard pressed to find a greater example of a pocket player than Bob Babbitt. He had the uncanny ability to create bass hooks—concise and funky lines that act as the defining element of the song. On tunes such as "Cool Jerk," Babbitt settles into an iconic line that locks in with the drums and percussion to create an irresistibly danceable groove. He masterfully integrates rhythmic variation while maintaining the integrity and feel of the song.

Babbitt didn't always play by the traditional rules of bass playing (aka, hitting on the downbeats). Instead, he added to the rhythmic complexity of a song by anticipating, pushing, or playing a dead note on beat one. Many of his Motown and soul recordings feature bass lines that rely on a specific and syncopated rhythmic pattern.

In addition to being completely comfortable and creative in the studio, Babbitt's greatest asset as a player was his understanding of when and how to implement variation. When it was time to pedal the root, he pedaled the root. When the bass groove stayed in one place while other instruments change parts, his handle on the hook was unyielding. But when he had an opportunity to stretch out, he demonstrated a keen knowledge of voice leading and melody.

Where Can I Hear Him?
"Midnight Train to Georgia"
Gladys Knight and the Pips, *Imagination*
Babbitt takes a very active approach to the bass line by playing heavily syncopated lines and weaving between registers. While many players pick a specific range to define a part, Babbitt jumps back and forth from the higher and lower octaves relating to the chords. He adds a counter-intuitive pulse on the up-beats throughout the song and perfectly executes diatonic voice leading as he transitions to the top of the verses.

"The Rubberband Man"
The Spinners, *Happiness Is Being With The Spinners*

The quintessential test for any great bass player is playing eighth notes that are straight up funky! This soul classic is the perfect example of pocket; throughout most of the record, Babbitt pulses eighth notes and discretely adds octave hiccups during the choruses to intensify the groove. I dare you not to dance.

"Scorpio"
Dennis Coffey and the Detroit Guitar Band, *Evolution*

Every now and then, an artist or producer decides it's a good idea to feature a bass solo on a record. Babbitt's approach to this bass break is a great example of development, space, and phrasing in a groove-based solo. He often rests between restating the initial groove of the song and adding funky embellishments, allowing the listener to hang on between phrases with great expectations of what is to come. Over the course of the solo, he builds momentum with busier rhythmic lines and finally ushers in the rest of the ensemble to return to the head of the tune.

Duck Dunn

An afro, a pipe, and a Precision—the definition of cool. Duck Dunn epitomized what it means to be a bass player with his simple, elegant, and superbly funky grooves.

Who Is Duck Dunn?
Born and raised in Memphis, Tennessee, Duck Dunn is best known as a member of Booker T. and The MG's, the house band at Stax studios. After going to high school with Steve Cropper, Dunn was brought in to work in the studio alongside Al Jackson and Booker T. Jones in 1964. The group served as the backing band for artists recording at Stax, most notably Otis Redding, Wilson Pickett, Sam and Dave, Eddie Floyd, Albert King, Isaac Hayes, and The Staple Singers. Booker T. and the MG's also enjoyed success with instrumental tunes including "Hang 'em High" and "Time is Tight."

    Throughout his career, Dunn also laid down the groove for Freddie King, Elvis Presley, Jerry Lee Lewis, John Prine, Rod

Stewart, Eric Clapton, Tom Petty, Bob Dylan, and many others. He was inducted to the Rock & Roll Hall of Fame, received a Grammy Lifetime Achievement Award, and was awarded Bass Player Magazine's Lifetime Achievement Award. As if that weren't enough, he was the uber-cool bass player in the Blues Brothers Band and can be seen in both the original movie and the sequel, Blues Brothers 2000. Duck Dunn passed away in May of 2012 at the age of 70 after a series of performances in Tokyo.

Let's Talk Style

When it comes to blues and soul music, Dunn's style was quite specific. Many of those tunes are part based, where each instrument plays a distinctive line. The individual components, such as the "chink" of a guitar, the horn stabs, and the bass groove, all come together like a musical puzzle. While his Motown contemporary, James Jamerson, had an improvisatory style and highly varied harmonic approach, Duck Dunn frequently settled into a repetitive hook to define the song. This approach became the standard for electric blues at the time, likely inspired by Willie Dixon's upright playing on the earlier Chess recordings.

On most of the hit soul records, there's little variation from the original groove, save for a few fills. Duck's soul grooves tended to be pentatonic in nature while his blues patterns often outlined the arpeggio or stuck to the root, octave, 5_{th}, and $b7_{th}$ on lick-based tunes. His overall style, though rather simplistic, was undeniably appropriate for the song, the singer, and the soloist.

As an ensemble player, Duck Dunn masterfully demonstrated how to groove with a band and make a record that relies upon feel. Most of the tunes recorded at Stax featured the rhythm section tracking together in the same room, giving the players the ability to communicate, lock in with one another, and establish a groove that resonates with the listener. Dunn drove the band with his affirmative tone, his willingness to hang back or push ahead with the other players, and his ability to follow the vocalist's interpretation of the song.

Where Can I Hear Him?
"Dock of the Bay" Otis Redding
One of the most iconic bass intros in classic rhythm and blues, Dunn's distinctive tone helps to set the mood of the record. He takes a root-5_{th} approach throughout most of the song, anchoring the music with a simple part that supports the lyrics. He pedals through the bridge to accompany the heightened energy of the vocals and then returns to the original theme to create the perfect backdrop for the memorable whistle outro.

"Born Under a Bad Sign"
Albert King, *Born Under A Bad Sign*

While the entire record *Born Under A Bad Sign* is a quintessential example of blues bass playing, the title track is well known for its hook. Dunn mimics the guitar riff at many points during the song but breaks away with a slightly different pattern during the verses. As a part, it is simple, definitive, and perfectly complementary to the main guitar line.

"She Caught the Katy"
The Blues Brothers Band, *The Blues Brothers*

This tune features a more active bass line, especially when compared to many early soul records. Duck grooves during the verses, uses a funky octave climb to the four chord, and even integrates a quick diminished riff. At the end of the song, the bass plays a chromatic descending line on the up-beats and is accompanied by some truly stanky horns.

David Hood

Think about your favorite bass line. Picture yourself hearing it on the radio: you're driving a car and suddenly, the perfect groove begins pulsating from the speakers. At that moment, you bop your head, tap your fingers, and forget about where you're going. You don't worry about the work at the office, the chores at home, getting to the bank before it closes, or what you're making for dinner. All you do is enjoy the music. When I think about some of *my* favorite bass lines, I realize that many of them originate in the same place. That place is Muscle Shoals and that bass player is David Hood.

Who Is David Hood?

Hailing from Sheffield, Alabama, David Hood has spent most of his life involved in the music scene of Muscle Shoals. First picking up guitar, he switched to bass at age 16 and gravitated towards rhythm and blues records. Inspired by artists like Ray Charles, Chuck Berry, and Jimmy Reed, Hood joined a local band, The Mystics. The band decided to make a record with Rick Hall at

FAME studios and a few years later, Hood got a call to play bass on a Percy Sledge session. This quickly turned into more phone calls for session work with soul and R&B artists like Aretha Franklin, Etta James, Wilson Pickett, Johnnie Taylor, and Clarence Carter.

In 1969, David Hood and fellow rhythm section players Barry Beckett, Roger Hawkins, and Jimmy Johnson, decided to break away from FAME studios. They opened Muscle Shoals Sound at 3614 Jackson Highway and began attracting artists from all over the country, including Cher, Paul Simon, Bob Seger, Laura Nyro, Leon Russell, Eddie Floyd, and Levon Helm, among others. Known as "The Swampers" (as referenced in Lynyrd Skynyrd's "Sweet Home Alabama"), the Muscle Shoals Rhythm Section played as a unit and adapted their style to fit the song, session, and artist. While most of his musical life has been spent in the studio, Hood toured with Traffic throughout the United States and Europe during the early 1970s. David Hood still resides in Muscle Shoals and frequently finds himself in the recording studio.

Let's Talk Style

As a full-time session player, Hood typically worked for artists and producers that specifically sought out the Muscle Shoals Rhythm Section. They were accountable for contributing to the music in an inventive, focused, and timely manner, and gained a reputation for doing so. Hood and the MSRS became masters at this, working collaboratively to play for the song.

With a remarkable sense of time and feel, Hood is one of the ultimate "pocket players," locking in perfectly with Roger Hawkins' groove behind the drum kit. On soul and R&B records, Hood crafts a simple yet catchy part, usually based on the pentatonic scale or the box pattern. "I'll Take You There" is perhaps the best-known example of Hood's steady and consistent execution of a memorable bass part, one that doesn't need fills or improvisation to keep the attention of the listener. Lucky for us, this song does spotlight him for a moment with a graceful and singable solo.

Working primarily in the studio rather than on the stage, he plays with keen attention to the impact of every note, knowing full well that he will soon be listening to a playback. His approach is rarely busy; he plays with a "less is more" mindset. Hood restrains from gratuitous fills and leaves space for other players, musical hooks, and vocalists to shine. Sessions with songwriters like Paul Simon required playing to the vision of the artist and the specific song arrangement. Simon's song "Kodachrome" features Hood following the chord changes with solid half notes, joining the instrumental hooks during the verse, driving the choruses with a bouncy triad groove, and throwing in quick voice leading lines. It's hard to imagine a better approach to playing such a song. His attention to detail, easy-going attitude, and inherent musicality are reasons enough to call him for a session.

Where Can I Hear Him?

"Warm and Tender Love" Percy Sledge

This track was David Hood's first call as a session player at FAME. His precision, consistency, and feel are clear indicators of his future in the studio. He executes a simple and soulful bass line that seamlessly locks in with the drummer, providing the perfect sway for slow-dancing couples. Derived from the major pentatonic scale, this is an ideal example of a '60s style Southern R&B groove—it remains consistent throughout the song and transposes the same pattern to every chord.

"My Little Town"
Paul Simon, *Still* Crazy *After All These Years*

Paul Simon had traveled to Muscle Shoals to record his previous record, *There Goes Rhymin' Simon,* and decided to call upon the MSRS once again. David Hood demonstrates sincere reverence for song arrangement by creating parts dictated by the form and instrumentation. He often plays in sync with the lower register of the piano and the horn section, at times enhancing the impact of the chord changes by using inversions. Gliding through the song with slick voice leading, he adds rhythmic accents with quick triplet flourishes and playful root-5_{th}-octave moves. As if that weren't enough, he executes a catchy descending melodic line during the chorus and outro, infusing the song with a truly memorable musical motif.

"(Sometimes I Feel So) Uninspired"
Traffic, *On The Road*

While still busy as a session player, Hood and the "The Swampers" joined Traffic for a few tours of the US and Europe in the mid-1970s. This live recording features him as the incomparable groove master, providing solid tone and a steady foundation for the other players to jam over. He executes beautiful voice leading and melodic counterpoint during the verses and plays with an acute sense of dynamics and drive throughout the solo sections.

Tommy Cogbill

Tommy Cogbill is one of the unsung heroes from the era of 1960s soul and R&B. A guitarist-turned-bass player, he provided the bottom end for many of the soul classics we know and love. Jumping from sessions in Memphis to Muscle Shoals, Nashville, and New York, his contributions as a bass player and producer have made the world a funkier place.

Who Is Tommy Cogbill?
A native of Johnson Grove, Tennessee, Tommy Cogbill took to the guitar at a young age and eventually made his way toward the electric bass. In the mid 1960s, he began picking up sessions in Memphis with a group that included Gene Chrisman on drums, Chips Moman and Reggie Young on guitar, and Bobby Emmons on keys. Often hired by Jerry Wexler for artists on Atlantic records, the group traveled to many of the famed studios (FAME, included) to achieve the appropriate sound and vibe for the artist. While he frequently recorded at American Sound Studios (owned by Chips

Moman), he's one of the few bass players from that era who regularly bounced around and didn't just stay at one studio. By the late 1960s, he had recorded with artists including Wilson Pickett, Aretha Franklin, Dusty Springfield, and Elvis Presley, among others.

Cogbill soon began stretching his muscles as a producer with The Box Tops, Arthur Alexander, and most notably, Neil Diamond. His bass playing and production work on "Sweet Caroline" speak for themselves. In addition to producing, he continued his career as a bass player throughout the 1970s and recorded with country artists and singer songwriters including Kris Kristofferson, J.J. Cale, Bob Seger, Jimmy Buffett, and Townes Van Zandt. Cogbill passed away in 1982 at the age of 50 due to a stroke.

Let's Talk Style

As we examine the bass lines of soul music makers from the 1960s, it's easy to see how certain players favor one another. Duck Dunn and David Hood have similar styles, as they are both meat-and-potato players who often find a simple groove or hook and maintain it throughout the song. Their lines are clean, consistent, and definitive. Other players, such as James Jamerson and Tommy Cogbill, are a bit more outgoing and improvisational. They establish a theme to play *to* and *around,* usually sneaking in creative fills, dead notes, and rhythmically busy lines. While Cogbill was dexterous enough to play intricate and imaginative lines, his respect for the song and genre always guided his performance.

Cogbill's overall musicality was impressive. His timing was dead-on, as demonstrated by his keen attention to note duration and the accuracy of his muting and attack. His experience on guitar no doubt translated well to the bass; he played the neck with freedom, knowing how certain notes would translate in the higher register of the instrument. His understanding of harmony was revealed when he navigated through chords in clever ways, frequently using the pentatonic scale as a roadmap and rarely shying away from highlighting the 7_{th} or 9_{th} of a chord. Furthermore, his placement of fills and melodic lines seemed completely natural as he took advantage of the space left between vocal lines and played to the listener's sense of musical symmetry.

Where Can I Hear Him?
"Son Of A Preacher Man"
Dusty Springfield, *Dusty In Memphis*
What makes this track so remarkable is the concept of movement; Cogbill's bass line provides a sense of motion and counter melody while most of the other instruments hold down a static foundation. The drums are solid and steady, the guitar and organ make a harmonic bed, and the horns respond to Springfield's vocal. Meanwhile, the bass is the instrument that moves. Bouncing between the root, 5_{th}, and octave, he throws in the 6_{th}, $b7_{th}$, and 9_{th} to

add tension. Cogbill opens up at the end of the song with major-pentatonic lines that ascend the neck and jump out of the mix.

"I Never Loved A Man (The Way I Love You)" Aretha Franklin, *I Never Loved A Man The Way I Love You*

Cogbill's approach to this song is like "Bass Playing 101." Come in at the right time with simple, yet definitive notes; hang back during the verses but provide direction when moving from chord to chord; use rhythm to bring up the dynamics when going to the bridge; and open up at the end of the song to match the intensity of the vocalist and other players. Cogbill executes perfect chromatic lines, skillfully directs the band back down to the root at the end of the phrase, and masterfully contributes to the changes in dynamics.

"Who Do You Love" Townes Van Zandt, *Flyin' Shoes*

Anyone who can make quarter notes groove as well as Cogbill does on this record is worthy of note. His timing is spot on with the kick drum. While the song remains on the same chord, his use of fills and pick-up notes create enough motion to separate the verses from the choruses. Playfully using the minor pentatonic scale, Cogbill executes slick descending lines on even bars (usually the second or fourth bar of a phrase). He takes the energy up a notch towards the end of the song by playing eighth notes, a simple choice that elevates the vamp out and reinforces the groove.

Leroy Hodges

While most of us associate early Memphis rhythm and blues with Sun Records or Stax, another studio began churning out hits around the same time with an intensely funky group of players: Royal Studios and the Hi Rhythm Section. Bringing a sophisticated and syncopated groove to Al Green and Ann Peebles records, Leroy Hodges is known for his long tenure at Royal Studios and his contributions to Southern soul music.

Who Is Leroy Hodges?
Leroy Hodges and his brothers, Teenie and Charles, grew up playing together in Memphis, Tennessee. In the late 1950s, they played with their father's band, The Germantown Dots, and later formed their own group, The Impalas. They eventually met Willie Mitchell, a trumpeter, bandleader, and soon-to-be producer for Hi Records. Mitchell put a house band together with the Hodges Brothers, Al Jackson Jr. (of Stax and Booker T and the MG's), and the Memphis Horns. The brothers began focusing on studio work

in the early 1970s, working out of Royal Studios with Mitchell writing and producing.

With Teenie on guitar, Charles on organ, and Leroy on bass, the Hodges brothers recorded on countless records as the Hi Rhythm Section. Accompanied by horns, strings, and multiple background parts, the production was quite different compared to the records coming out of Stax. With hits by Al Green, Ann Peebles, Otis Clay, Syl Johnson, and many others, they wrote a new chapter in the book of Southern soul music. Hodges' career experienced a bit of resurgence in the 2000s as artists like Melissa Etheridge and Robert Cray sought out old-school session cats and the authentic "Memphis Sound."

Let's Talk Style

As we discuss some of the great jazz players, we often say "man, that cat really *swings.*" Such a player walks through changes and defines time alongside a dancing ride cymbal, pushing the song along with quarter notes that magically imply a triplet feel. As we listen to the great R&B players, we try to quantify the same thing, though it feels a bit awkward to say, "man, that cat really... souls?" Of course, the music can swing, but it can also shuffle, be played straight, or give birth to a new kind of feel. The bass players behind the R&B records of the '60s and '70s give life to a song by committing to a specific bass line or pulse, one that attaches to the kick drum while leaving space for the rhythm guitar and organ stabs. Their playing is difficult to replicate since their note duration is unique. They force us to move our bodies and crinkle our noses in response to the so-called stank of the Memphis shuffle. So, if there's one player that really "souls," it's Leroy Hodges.

Listening to some of the great Al Green records, you may notice that Hodges creates catchy and effective grooves for different sections of a song. He switches up the bass pattern to complement the melody and song form, even while other members of the rhythm section adhere to the original part.

In addition to Hodges' impeccable feel and rhythmic aptitude, his deep understanding of harmony is evident in the way he moves through chord progressions. He constantly experiments with ways to approach the root of a chord; sometimes he arrives by way of the lower 5_{th}, the 3_{rd}, the whole step above, or the half step below. He uses quick triplet fills, often slipping in a "2-#2-3" lick to lift the song and highlight the 3_{rd} of the chord. This playful attention to the 3_{rd} also factors into his grooves and hooks, particularly as he emphasizes the minor 3_{rd} over a 7_{th} chord to give the song a bluesier character.

Where Can I Hear Him?
"Let's Stay Together" Al Green, *Let's Stay Together*
A breakthrough hit for Al Green, this song features a deceptively complex bass line that integrates soulful arpeggios, voice leading, quick string raking, and the musical brightness of 10_{th} chords.

Hodges' use of rhythmic variation and fills are Jamersonian in nature, though his personal approach and laid-back feel set him apart.

"You Got Me Comin'" Hi Rhythm Band, *On The Loose*

This tune starts out with a sped-up version of the tape with the bass and drums high in the mix. It quickly winds down to the original track and reveals the rhythm section we're used to hearing on records like "Take Me To The River." Hodges provides a steady pulse, a well-defined root-6_{th}-5_{th} bass groove, and a textbook R&B tone.

"I Can't Stand The Rain"
Ann Peebles, *I Can't Stand The Rain*

The title track on a seriously funky record, Hodges creates a simple and solid bass hook using the root and minor 3_{rd}. Rounding it out with a chromatic triplet line, he acts as the perfect complement to the drummer's steady groove. During the verses, he provides a slightly irregular, yet absolutely perfect pulse: rather than playing straight eighth notes, he varies the number of times he attacks a note. Although this method is somewhat improvisational, he continues to anchor the song by emphasizing the kick drum pattern.

George Porter, Jr.

A name synonymous with New Orleans funk, George Porter, Jr. is widely known for his swampy and soulful bass playing. A longtime member of The Meters and a first-call session cat, he speaks volumes with a single note played in just the right place. Donning an authentically worn Fender Precision and often a tie-dye shirt, he playfully reflects the New Orleans motto "laissez les bons temps rouler" in his appearance and music alike.

Who Is George Porter, Jr.?
A native of New Orleans, Louisiana, Porter grew up in a musical family, exposed to church choirs, jazz, and traditional bayou music. Initially playing rhythm guitar, he made the switch to bass after a few lessons from another local bass player, Benjamin "Poppi" Francis. At a young age, Porter developed a friendship with drummer Joe "Zigaboo" Modeliste and the two began jamming and playing gigs around town. They soon met Aaron Neville and were asked to join his band, Neville Sound. Many local club gigs and a

few lineup changes later, the core group of Aaron Neville, Zigaboo Modeliste, Leo Nocentelli, and George Porter, Jr. signed a record deal with producer Allen Toussaint and changed their name to The Meters.

During the early to mid-'70s, The Meters released a handful of records and hit the road, eventually opening for the Rolling Stones in 1975. During this time, Toussaint also called upon Porter and other members of The Meters to play on record dates for artists such as Lee Dorsey, Robert Palmer, and Dr. John. Although The Meters decided to part ways in 1977, various members have reunited over the years, adopting names such as The Funky Meters and The Original Meters.

After the initial breakup of The Meters, Porter formed the band Joyride and continued to do session work. He can be heard on records by Taj Mahal, Tori Amos, John Scofield, Patti LaBelle, Albert King, David Byrne, Warren Haynes, Robbie Robertson, and many others. Through the early 2000s he continued to tour with The Runnin Pardners, The Funky Meters, and various other projects.

Let's Talk Style
As I frequently revisit The Meters' catalogue, I can't help but notice the greatest groove-inducing element: space. Porter usually begins with a distinctive line, often just a few notes, enhanced by the accompanying swing of the rhythm guitar. The simple phrase leaves

room for organ embellishments and the highly syncopated, second-line inspired drums and percussion ("Fire On The Bayou" and "People Say" are great examples of this). His mature and minimalist approach is the basis for many of the hit instrumental tunes from the group—he functions as the foundation of the groove, the roux of the gumbo.

From a harmonic standpoint, Porter's approach to songs with a major tonality frequently pulls from a "bayou-ized" version of an arpeggio with the addition of the 6_{th}. This is common pattern in blues and Zydeco (a traditional Louisiana/Cajun genre). He adds glissandos or half-step pickups as he moves through the major pentatonic scale. In doing so, he create tension, particularly when adding a chromatic triplet line from the 2_{nd} scale degree. More often than not, Porter creates a groove simply using the root, 5_{th}, and 7_{th}, leaving plenty of room for harmonic interpretation by the soloists and intricate fills that flirt with 3_{rds}. This provides him with an interesting advantage; he can choose to pronounce the $b3_{rd}$ to firmly dictate a minor tonality or to add bluesy dissonance. Similarly, he can emphasize the major 3_{rd} over a 9_{th} or $\#9_{th}$ chord to brighten the overall harmonic feel.

Where Can I Hear Him?
"Hey Pocky A-Way" The Meters, *Rejuvenation*
Kicking off with Zigaboo's signature New Orleans-style groove, Porter enters the mix with an attention-grabbing lick. He relies

heavily on "gulping" slides as he jumps registers and casually brushes a seventh chord double stop before settling into the trademark bass line of the song. Maintaining a consistent groove through all of the verses, Porter exemplifies the concept of space with a two-bar phrase that leaves the last two beats open. This creates anticipation for the return of the bass and allows space for horn stabs and a single percussive clap on beat four.

"Cissy Strut/Soul Island/You're The One" The Funky Meters, *Fiyo at the Fillmore*

This particular track is a great window into Porter's live playing. With more improvisation and wiggle room, the band plays a medley beginning with their best-known hit, "Cissy Strut." Porter takes a heavily punctuated and staccato approach to the notes and lets loose during the jam and solo section. Relying heavily on the root, 5_{th}, and 2_{nd}, he outlines the harmony of a 9_{th} chord but leaves space for the funky interpretation of the major and minor 3_{rd}. He settles into another groove theme towards the end of the jam, accenting the 6_{th} and $b7_{th}$ to heighten the dynamic solo section before returning to the main theme. Jumping into the next tune, "Soul Island," the band is ushered in by Porter's rhythmic pulses on the root followed by distinctly Caribbean-feeling major arpeggios. Toward the end of this section of the medley, Porter plays a syncopated harmony line to accompany the lead guitar before transitioning to "You're The One."

"Sneakin' Sally Through The Alley"
Robert Palmer, *Sneakin' Sally Through The Alley*

As the title track to Robert Palmer's debut solo record, Porter begins the groove with staccato stabs on the root, octave and $b7_{th}$. He interacts with the percussive keyboard part and leaves space for the snare accents on beats two and four. After following the chord changes, he concludes the groove structure with a funky lick stemming from the 4_{th} and leading straight back to the punches on the root. Although there is little, if any, variation in the bass line, he carries the track with his swampy feel and the clever signature lick.

Section II:

The Band

Jack Bruce

During the British Invasion of the 1960s, Cream rose to the top as the quintessential power trio. The album *Disraeli Gears* showcases Eric Clapton's wailing guitar solos, Ginger Baker's innovative drumming, and Jack Bruce's overdriven bass lines. The creative contributions of each member proved integral to the style, sound, and personality of the band. Their music continues to be a timeless staple of classic rock repertoire and Jack Bruce will forever live on as a bass player to know.

Who Is Jack Bruce?
Widely recognized for his work with Cream, Jack Bruce had an amazing career both as a band member and solo artist. Hailing from Glasgow, Scotland, Bruce grew up in a musical family. He began life as a classically trained player, specializing in bass, cello, and composition, and briefly attended the Royal Scottish Academy of Music. Following school, he moved to London, dove into the rock and blues scene, and met drummer Ginger Baker. During the early

to mid-'60s, he played with a number of artists, including Alexis Korner, Graham Bond, John Mayall, and Manfred Mann. After meeting Eric Clapton while playing with John Mayall, Bruce joined with Clapton and Ginger Baker to form the band Cream. The group released a handful of albums, including *Fresh Cream, Disraeli Gears,* and *Wheels Of Fire,* which became the first ever platinum-selling double album. Although they disbanded in 1968, they made a strong mark both locally and internationally with their fusion of traditional blues and amped up rock and roll.

Following the breakup of Cream, Jack Bruce devoted time to his solo material, releasing his first record, *Songs For A Tailor,* in 1969. Throughout his career, he has recorded and toured with other artists, including Lou Reed, Frank Zappa, Robin Trower, Ringo Starr and His All-Starr Band, Mose Allison, and Kip Hanrahan. He also has roughly a dozen records as a solo artist. Bruce was inducted into the Rock & Roll Hall of Fame and received the Grammy Lifetime Achievement Award as a member of Cream. He passed away in 2014 due to liver disease.

Let's Talk Style

If you had to pick one word to define Jack Bruce's modus operandi, it would be intensity. This doesn't mean that every song is a heavy-hitting up-tempo number, but that his bass lines are up front, deliberate, and enthusiastic. His tone has a similar positive charge; Bruce wasn't afraid to push the envelope or the overdrive to be heard. He tended to be mid-range centric, which works well in a power trio and gives plenty of definition to the bass lines that carry the tune. He had less than conventional taste when it came to instruments, going from a Fender Bass VI to a Gibson EB-3 to a fretless Warwick, which further set his style apart from other bass players.

Jack Bruce's musical contributions, both with Cream and as a solo artist, reflect the luxury of creative freedom. Most of the Cream material was written by, for, and around the specific players and instrumentation, allowing each of the players to showcase their talents and play off one another. While their music is rooted in traditional forms, such as a twelve-bar blues, they managed to take a creative approach to harmony. By adding hints of dissonance, playing with the pentatonic scale, and using syncopated rhythms, they embraced psychedelia while maintaining the song form.

Once he stepped out of Cream, Bruce's solo work was a fusion of rock, jazz, and blues with nods to his background in classical composition. Transitions from one section to another are frequently marked by a classical string section approach, using voice leading and counterpoint to give direction. He continued to maintain his signature tone and strong-willed vocals throughout his catalogue, further enforcing his intensity and creative will as an artist.

Where Can I Hear Him?
"Badge" Cream, *Goodbye*

Jack Bruce's catchy and iconic bass line serves as the signature hook of the song, integrating space, groove, and classical inspiration. The bass line supports the melody while outlining the chord structure—a great example of soprano-bass counterpoint. Furthermore, he does a masterful job of leading the song from section to section. Take a listen to the quick descending line at the end of the verse; both the phrasing and note choice nod to a transition reminiscent of a classical symphony.

"Never Tell Your Mother She's Out of Tune"
Jack Bruce, *Songs For A Tailor*

Bruce taps into a number of different grooves by traversing between a funky root pedal, a walking blues pattern, and a descending hook with a triplet feel. Again, this is a great example of his tremendous intensity; Bruce's midrange-heavy tone allows him to stand out in the mix, adding extra edge to his aggressive eighth note pulses.

"Politician"
Cream, *Royal Albert Hall: London May 2-3-4-5-6 2005*

This dark and psychedelic tune represents the timeless nature of the blues. Recorded at the band's long-awaited reunion show in 2005, it features Bruce on the vocals and as the groove master. While Bruce is fairly "chilled out" compared to other performances, he provides a strong and supportive foundation that relies on space, intentionality, and a bit of dissonance. He adds movement to the solo section by elaborating on the groove and playing the original theme in the higher register.

Bill Wyman

While the quote "It's Only Rock 'N' Roll But I Like It" has become a bit trite, there's no denying the fact that, like many clichés, it is often true. It requires a certain amount of raw talent, part-driven playing, and soulful swagger to play in one of the greatest rock and roll bands of all time. As an integral member of The Rolling Stones and the bass player on the hits we all love, Bill Wyman is a bass player to know.

Who Is Bill Wyman?
On December 7, 1962, Bill Wyman managed to find himself in an interesting musical scenario: he showed up to play with a few other lads in London, hit it off, and began a 31-year stint with The Rolling Stones. Hailing from Lewisham, Wyman joined the Stones after being introduced by then-drummer, Tony Chapman. Shortly after Wyman became part of the band, Charlie Watts replaced Chapman and the Stones as we know them began writing, recording and performing their unique blend of blues, R&B, and rock and

roll. In addition to playing on the Stones' classic albums, Wyman concentrated on solo projects from the mid-1970s onward, including the self-titled *Bill Wyman*, *Monkey Grip*, and *A Stone Alone*.

After three decades with the band, Wyman decided to leave the group in 1993 to pursue other projects, including photography, writing, and new musical endeavors. He formed "Bill Wyman's Rhythm Kings" in 1996 and began writing, recording, and touring. Wyman has published an autobiography and a book of photography documenting his experiences with The Rolling Stones. He continues to work on various artistic projects.

Let's Talk Style

Working through the catalogue of Stones records, I can't help but relate the band's uniquely crafted rock and roll tunes to one of the great wonders of the culinary world: pizza. Charlie Watts is the foundation—the crust—providing the trusty and solid bed upon which everything sits. Mick Jagger supplies the gooey elastic vocal line that entices the consumer (the cheesy goodness, if you will). Keith Richards provides the toppings—the unique flavor and delectable licks that define each song. And last but not least, Bill Wyman is the sauce. He lies just below the surface, sinks into the crust, and supplies the delightful tang and "*je ne sais quoi*" that elevates the perfect slice of pie.

Wyman has an innate sense of musicality that makes him the ideal bass player for The Rolling Stones. He understands how to lock in with Watts, complement the rhythm guitar, leave space at the appropriate moments, and support the song with solid root notes, primal energy, and traditional blues patterns. Wyman tends to settle into bass *parts* as opposed to bass *lines;* he doesn't necessarily play a set groove or sequence of notes. Instead, he establishes a somewhat loose, yet clearly distinguishable part that unites all the musical elements of the song. His part is malleable and reactive, always going with the flow of the band and often developing in complexity as the song progresses.

Playing with a distinctively "rooted" mindset, Wyman clearly defines the harmony of the song, which happens to be just the right thing for rock and roll. He inherently knows the perfect moment to jump up an octave, creating a sense of motion even though the harmony remains the same. Though his approach is fairly simplistic in terms of note choice, he has a keen understanding of how to drive a song with low-register power.

Where Can I Hear Him?
"Monkey Man" The Rolling Stones, *Let It Bleed*
Wyman kicks this song off with a funky, octave-based groove as the atmosphere builds and develops before the verse. He rides the root during most of the song, often jumping up the octave to supply movement, and wavers between punctuating the rhythm guitar and

locking in with Watts. As the song progresses, he takes a loose and varied approach regarding *when* and *what* to play, sometimes dropping out during long sections and favoring slides and sounds as opposed to distinctive notes.

"It's A Wonder" Bill Wyman, *Monkey Grip*

In case you've ever wondered whether Wyman can bring the funk, check out this grooving tune from his 1974 solo effort. With a handful of odd bars thrown in, this song leaves the listener waiting in anticipation of the thunderous re-entrance after each break. Evolving into a jam over a I-to-IV chord progression, Wyman soulfully slides between the two chords, jumps registers to embellish with fills, and introduces variations to the original groove.

"Love Letters" Bill Wyman's Rhythm Kings, *The Collectors Edition Box Set*

A modern take on an R&B classic, this song is a great example of *why* Wyman started the Rhythm Kings: it is a musical outlet to play the songs he wants to play with the people he wants to play them with. His approach is simple, elegant, and shows great respect for traditional rhythm and blues.

Rick Danko

As a solo artist, accompanist, and legendary low-end driver of The Band, Rick Danko has made an indelible mark on popular music. Known for supporting Bob Dylan during the early days of going electric, his contributions as a bass player, vocalist, and fiddle player continue to resonate in the world of folk-inspired music.

Who Is Rick Danko?
Born in Ontario, Canada, he was inspired by country, rhythm and blues, and gospel music. As a teenager, he left school to pursue a playing career and quickly joined Ronnie Hawkins' band, The Hawks, as the rhythm guitarist. Danko made the transition to bass and toured throughout the early 1960s with Band-to-be members Levon Helm and Robbie Robertson. In 1964, this group of players left Ronnie Hawkins' band and were contacted by Bob Dylan about going on the road. They joined Dylan as his backing band from 1965 through 1967 and gained notoriety under their new name, The Band.

The Band released *Music From Big Pink* (1968), named after the house they inhabited in Woodstock after touring with Dylan. They followed it with their second album, *The Band*. Both records featured Danko as a vocalist, taking lead on a handful of songs and adding harmony parts. After roughly a decade of writing and touring, members of The Band decided to move on to other projects and produced a famous farewell concert and film, *The Last Waltz*, in 1977.

After leaving The Band, Danko continued to tour, write, and release music. In addition to his solo records, he collaborated with folk artists Eric Andersen and Jonas Fjeld, participated in revivals of The Band, and toured with Ringo Starr's All-Starr Band. As a session player, he has contributed to records by Neil Young, Joe Cocker, and Emmylou Harris. Danko passed away due to heart failure in December 1999, just before his 56th birthday.

Let's Talk Style

Living up to the musical standard set by the name The Band isn't easy—it implies that the group of players isn't just *a* band, rather *the* band. In other words, they must be exceptional at playing music together. As a writer, vocalist, bass player, and all-around musician, Rick Danko was essential in defining the sound of this ensemble.

First and foremost, Danko was an accompanist who knew how to let the whole be greater than the sum of its parts. Alongside Levon Helm, Danko fostered a deep understanding of rhythmic interplay. As a rhythm section, they intuitively supported one another by providing space for fills, accentuating downbeats, and dynamically opening up the song together (e.g., Danko playing longer notes with Helm switching from hi-hat to ride). You'd be hard-pressed to find stronger quarter notes than those driving songs like "The Shape I'm In," where the energy of both players hitting together creates a simple yet effective groove.

Danko also had a keen ear for picking up on melodic elements and often mimicked the vocal melody or lead line played by the keys, guitar, or horns. He jumped back and forth between playing a bass groove and syncing with other instruments, always demonstrating his knowledge of other players' parts and how he could re-enforce them to better the arrangement.

From the standpoint of harmony, Danko often took advantage of playing chord inversions to aid in voice leading or to add complexity to a stand-alone chord. Take a listen to the chorus of "The Night They Drove Old Dixie Down" or "The Weight," and you'll hear how he used the 5_{th} or 3_{rd} instead of the root to add color. Another interesting "Dankoism" is the intentional use of the half-step to lead into chords. He used this technique in "Up On Cripple Creek" by emphasizing the major 7_{th} before sliding into the root. This creates a swampy and elongated downbeat that reinforces the vibe of the song and adds weight (no pun intended) to the tonic chord.

Where Can I Hear Him?

"Life Is A Carnival" The Band, *The Last Waltz*

On one of the funkier numbers by The Band, Danko settles into a pentatonic-based groove that playfully converses with Levon Helm's kick drum pattern—they go back and forth between simultaneous hits and intentionally leaving space for one another. The groove supports complex horn lines, at times providing low-note stabs, and continuously emphasizes beat four throughout the song. During the choruses, Danko plays heavily pronounced quarter notes, creating a simple contrast to the groove of the verse. All in all, this tune is a perfect example of Danko's understanding of interplay and arrangement.

"Blue River" Danko, Fjeld, Andersen, *One More Shot*

Led by Danko's soulful and heartfelt vocals, this song features an eloquent and gentle bass part that emphasizes voice leading through chromatic movement and chord inversions. Rather than playing a particular groove, he sticks to an easy, half-note feel that settles in over the drums. He adds rhythmic embellishment by punctuating the more dynamic moments of the song and by mimicking the rhythm of the melody during the chorus.

"Knockin' On Heaven's Door"
Bob Dylan and The Band, *Before the Flood*

Danko takes a slightly busier approach to this song with punctuating staccato lines leading from chord to chord. He explores the range of the instrument by sliding to the higher octaves and then returning with descending pentatonic lines. During the choruses, he supports the vocal harmonies and adds playful licks between phrases.

Tom Hamilton

Whether it's the loud guitars, eccentric front men, or iconic songs, great rock and roll bands embody the sound, image, and appeal of cool. As a child of the '90s (when music videos still accounted for the majority of "music television" programming), there were few things cooler than the latest Aerosmith effort. Though lead singer Steven Tyler and guest actress Alicia Silverstone dominated most of the screen time, the powerful rhythm section and piercing guitars certainly inspired air drumming, mock guitar wailing, and, for a special few, pretend bass plucking. For bringing rock solid root notes and energetic, overdriven riffs to one of the most classic of classic rock bands, Aerosmith's Tom Hamilton is a bass player to know.

Who is Tom Hamilton?
Hailing from Colorado Springs, Colorado, Tom Hamilton took up the guitar at age 12 and switched to electric bass two years later. He found himself on the East Coast and joined a band with Joe Perry

named "The Jam Band." While playing in New Hampshire, Perry and Hamilton met Steven Tyler at a show and decided to combine their respective musical projects. They moved to Boston in 1970, and, after a few personnel changes, the group officially formed Aerosmith.

The band signed a record deal with Columbia Records in 1972 and released a self-titled debut album in 1973. 1975 introduced *Toys in the Attic*, which featured the band's first top-40 hit (and Hamilton composition) "Sweet Emotion," as well as "Walk This Way." At this point, the band officially took off and has since won multiple Grammy Awards, MTV Video Music Awards, and Billboard awards (just to name a few) and has been inducted into the Rock & Roll Hall of Fame. After many years of recording, touring, platinum albums, *Wayne's World* appearances, ups, downs, and everything in between, Aerosmith continues to sell out arenas and perform at the highest level.

Tom Hamilton, a consistent member of the group, hadn't missed an Aerosmith performance until 2006 when he was diagnosed with throat and tongue cancer. He has since undergone treatment and was able to rejoin the band for various tours and recording endeavors.

Let's Talk Style

Listening to Tom Hamilton, I can't help but recognize the perfect storm that is his playing: an ideal combination of bold, confident, and creative note choices with keen attention to form and arrangement. Much of the early Aerosmith material derives from blues and 1960s rock and roll, where the rhythm section drives the song with pedaling eighth notes, passing lines, and traditional blues patterns.

Some of his most creative and distinctive bass lines, including "Sweet Emotion," play with wide interval range and suspended chords. He uses open strings to create a low drone and then jumps to the higher register while allowing the low notes to ring out. Rather than sticking to just the 3_{rd}, 5_{th}, and octave, he creates melodic lines that favor the 4_{th}, 6_{th}, and 2_{nd} (or 9_{th}) scale degrees. His bass lines allude to the strumming of a suspended or altered chord (as if it were played on guitar) and, in addition to being the song's hook, they establish a feeling of space.

Hamilton is also a master of transitions. He clearly dictates the arrangement of the song, plays perfectly in sync with the drummer, and pinpoints the ideal place for a fill or transitional line. He slyly asserts his creativity with melodic riffs and register changes that signal a destination for the rest of the band, without ever overshadowing or competing with the other instruments.

Where Can I Hear Him?
"Cryin'" Aerosmith, *Get A Grip*
One word: Tone. Hamilton supports the song with strong, ballsy root notes that provide the perfect amount of "umph" to drive the

band. His flawless note choice and impeccable timing provide the ultimate foundation to make this a true power ballad. Finally, I would argue that it's hard to find better bass tone on a rock record.

"Uncle Salty" Aerosmith, *Toys In The Attic*

Kicking the song off with a creative, high-register melodic line, Hamilton jumps into the verse with a quarter note driven groove that acts as an extension of the theme. He effortlessly locks in with the drummer both rhythmically and dynamically. It's obvious that the band worked together on the arrangement of the song, as Hamilton provides intensity to complement the snare at the end of the verse before the song opens up with the ride cymbal, sustained notes, and vocal harmonies.

"Walk This Way" Aerosmith, *Toys in The Attic*

Arguably the most popular Aerosmith song, Hamilton has a striking and aggressive tone to complement his energetic bass line. If you've never listened closely to some of the fills between the phrases of the chorus and guitar solos, I urge you to do so. Hamilton sneaks in intricate and athletic fills that are easy to miss as we casually listen to the song over the radio, so keep your ears sharp and attuned to the sweeping minor pentatonic lines and chromatic triplets.

Paul Simonon

Spend an afternoon searching through the stacks of a record store and you may stumble upon a few iconic album covers: the colorful eclecticism of *Sgt. Pepper's Lonely Hearts Club Band*, the eerie prism of *Dark Side of The Moon,* or the adrenaline-enhanced act of destruction on *London Calling.* A Fender was, in fact, harmed in the making of that record—an epic sacrifice in the name of rock. While I never endorse the smashing of instruments, this image immortalized the raw passion and severity of The Clash's music and of bassist Paul Simonon. After digging in to more of The Clash's catalogue, as well as other records that featured Simonon's playing, it was easy to see that his gritty, reggae-inspired grooves make him a bass player to know.

Who Is Paul Simonon?
Hailing from Brixton, South London, Simonon was the son of an artist and librarian. With plenty of artistic aptitude, he originally attended the Byam Shaw School of Art and didn't pick up a bass

until the formation of The Clash. After meeting Mick Jones in 1976, and subsequently learning bass parts from him, the band began recording and performing their culturally relevant post-punk music. A show in New York City in 1979 resulted in the infamous cover image for *London Calling*, where Simonon destroyed a Fender Precision in a moment of frustration.

Over the course of the next ten years, The Clash ushered in a new era of rock that brought socio-economic commentary to the forefront of popular music. While they disbanded in 1986, Simonon continued to have a career as both an artist and musician. In addition to album artwork, design, and painting, his other musical projects include The Good, The Band and The Queen as well as Havana 3am. He can also be heard on Bob Dylan's record *Down in the Groove* and *Plastic Beach* by Gorillaz.

Let's Talk Style
While Simonon is not a particularly schooled player, his attitude and energetic performance style combine to create a dynamic personality. Influenced by the pronounced grooves of reggae music, most of his lines stem from syncopated major and minor arpeggios. He frequently drops the downbeat of a bar or creates short rhythmic phrases that act as a response to the melody or signature guitar lines.

In a live setting, his attention seems to be focused more on performance than precision. Although he can be somewhat erratic and sloppy, his passion for the music makes him a great entertainer.

Technique-wise, he is a forceful player, digging in with his thumb or using a pick to get a sharp, bright attack. This assertive style of playing drives the band. Thanks to his personality and the gritty tone of an overdriven Precision, The Clash is able to stand on the shoulders of Simonon's groove.

Where Can I Hear Him?
"The Guns Of Brixton" The Clash, *London Calling*
Featuring Simonon as writer, bass player, and lead vocalist, this song is a grungy, reggae-inspired commentary of cultural turmoil in Brixton, South London. The bass theme outlines a minor arpeggio, first ascending, then descending. The pattern barely wavers; it remains consistent throughout the song and becomes somewhat trance inducing when combined with the scratchy guitars and syncopated drums.

"Plastic Beach" Gorillaz, *Plastic Beach*
Simonon plays a dub-like, percussive part during the introduction of this track, providing just enough harmonic background for the swirling guitars and vibey noises. As the drums and vocals kick in, he alternates between two specific verse and chorus patterns, equally catchy in their rhythmic simplicity. He often remains silent

on the first beat of the measure, a classic reggae approach to bass playing, and effortlessly moves between the root-5th-octave of the chord.

"Kingdom of Doom" The Good, The Bad and The Queen
Simonon plays a pulsing root groove to complement the strumming guitars and provide both rhythmic and harmonic support. Without the aid of a full drum kit throughout most of the song, the groove is completely under his control. He often drops the first beat of the measure and mimics rhythmic elements of the vocal melody. His longer note duration matches the lyrical phrases of the chorus, creating a sense of space in this stripped-down instrumentation.

Cliff Burton

In four years and only three records, he created a legacy that lives on forever. I can think of no other bass player who has defined the style, sound, and attitude of a genre of music in the way Cliff Burton did. While most Bass Players To Know have extensive catalogues and diverse resumes, Burton's body of work was limited to a select number of recordings with a single entity, Metallica. His playing has become so widely celebrated and influential that he clearly deserves the same kind of praise reserved for the bass greats. His stellar technical ability, innovative approach, and musical contributions to Metallica make him one of the greatest players to ever pick up the instrument.

Who Is Cliff Burton?
Born in Castro Valley, California, Cliff Burton grew up listening to classical and popular music. He began playing bass as a teenager, forming bands throughout high school and college. All the while, he would practice for hours, noting Stanley Clark, Phil Lynott,

Geezer Butler, and Geddy Lee among his influences. In 1982, he joined the band Trauma and performed with them at the Whisky a Go Go in Los Angeles. Lars Ulrich and James Hetfield were in attendance and, after the performance, asked Burton to join Metallica. Burton joined the band on the condition that James and Lars would relocate to El Cerrito, California, and the two agreed.

With Burton as an official member of Metallica, the band recorded their debut album *Kill 'Em All* in 1983 on Megaforce Records. As their popularity grew, they released *Ride the Lightning* and grabbed the attention of Elektra Records. After signing their first major label deal, they released *Master of Puppets* in March of 1986 and embarked on an extensive tour in support of the record. While on the road in Sweden, a bus accident took the life of Cliff Burton on September 27th, 1986 at the age of 24.

Let's Talk Style
Burton exceled as a bass player in the traditional sense; he was the adhesive that kept the band together by smoothing out rhythmic inconsistencies, supporting the song harmonically, and mimicking or adding inflection to guitar riffs. His playing was controlled, intentional, and technically demanding. He provided the necessary low-end support that any reputable instrumentalist would, yet also managed to set a new standard for what is acceptable and expected of the bass player in the metal genre.

As an exceptional soloist and composer, his moment in the spotlight was celebrated and encouraged by both the audience and the other members of Metallica—so much so that it gave other bass players in the genre permission to have their own prominent voice instead of always standing in the background. His overdriven tone, use of effects, and adrenalized personality made him a captivating performer and essential member of the band. He cleverly integrated techniques often reserved for electric guitar, including bends, hammer-ons, and tapping, in a way that inspired a new generation of players to further explore the sonic potential of the instrument. By marrying classical harmonic development with testosterone-soaked improvisation, he showcased a mature sense of musicality while head banging, running around the stage, and exhibiting the commanding presence of the rock god he truly was.

Where Can I Hear Him?
"Anesthesia—Pulling Teeth" Metallica, *Kill 'Em All*
This performance will forever inspire bass players to add effects to their tone, favor chords and arpeggios as compositional elements, and bask in the spotlight while the rest of the band leaves the stage. He begins the composition by outlining the harmony in a controlled and deliberate manner. As the themes develop, he integrates melodic flourishes, bends, and chords until Lars joins the party. At that moment, the song kicks into higher gear with flurries

of notes, technically difficult riffs, register jumps, and screeching effects.

"For Whom The Bell Tolls"
Metallica, *Ride The Lightning*

One of the most iconic riffs in metal, Burton begins the song in the highest register of the instrument, accented by growling guitar chords and Lars' back beat. Burton then jumps down to the lowest register, playing a chromatic line from the b3_{rd} to the root. As the vocals kick in, he continues to support the song with dense chords and accents on beat two—an unconventional and creative approach that emphasizes Ulrichs' kick and snare.

"Orion" Metallica, *Master Of Puppets*

This piece has as much in common with classical composition as it does modern metal. It is an instrumental odyssey that begins with lush chords followed by accented guitar riffs, syncopated rhythms, composed guitar solos, and a bass breakdown. The band drops out as Burton establishes a new musical motif, outlining the harmony while adding quick embellishments. As the guitars provide wailing chords and additional melodic themes, they set up a perfectly composed moment of interplay. Alluding to traditional counterpoint, they play a harmonized line supported by melodic movement in the bass. This gives way to another solo section followed by a return to the original theme to remind you that you are, in fact, listening to heavy music.

Tina Weymouth

Few bands have a sound as instantly recognizable as the one created by Talking Heads. The combination of David Byrne's vocal tone, Brian Eno's production methods and, my personal favorite, Tina Weymouth's bass parts, make for records that have withstood the test of time. These leaders of the New Wave pop movement of the late 1970s and 1980s developed their unique approach using recently invented synth sounds, punchy bass lines, and clearly defined rhythmic parts. As the low-end anchor and cofounder of Talking Heads and Tom Tom Club, Tina Weymouth is a bass player to know.

Who Is Tina Weymouth?
Originally from California, Weymouth grew up alongside seven siblings with various artistic interests, including design, architecture, and music. A self-taught guitarist, she began playing music as a teenager and later decided to attend the Rhode Island School of Design. While attending school, she began dating fellow student

Chris Frantz, who had been playing drums in a band with David Byrne. By 1975, Weymouth, Frantz, and Byrne moved to New York City. At the suggestion of Frantz, Weymouth began playing bass to join what would soon be known as Talking Heads. The band released their first record, *Talking Heads: 77,* as well as their first single, "Psycho Killer," after signing a deal with Sire Records.

Between 1978 and 1980, Talking Heads released three records while collaborating with producer Brian Eno, resulting in commercial success and radio hits including "Take Me To The River," "Life During Wartime," and "Once In A Lifetime." By 1981, the band went on a hiatus, spurring solo efforts by Byrne and the formation of Tom Tom Club by Weymouth, her husband Frantz, and Weymouth's sisters. Tom Tom Club gained popularity with the single "Genius Of Love," solidifying their fresh sound and creative autonomy outside of Talking Heads.

Depending on the season, Weymouth continued to be an integral part of Talking Heads and Tom Tom Club, each band taking priority while the other took time off. While Talking Heads officially disbanded in the early 1990s, they retain a widespread influence over popular music and were inducted into the Rock & Roll Hall of Fame in 2002. Tom Tom Club continued to release records until 2012 and Weymouth briefly collaborated with other groups including Happy Mondays and Gorillaz.

Let's Talk Style

While some bass players make a living playing in a subtle and mellow manner, Weymouth does just the opposite. Instead of playing longer notes that provide a glue-like adhesion to the sound of a band, she manages to support the rhythm section with articulation, space, and acute attention to note duration. Her style reflects distinctive and syncopated notes with a tone that cuts through the mix, providing her own brand of boldness to Talking Heads and Tom Tom Club. Her playing and writing style is edgy—a product of pop, punk and modern art in the 1980s.

Weymouth embraces the essence of dance music, disco, reggae, and early hip-hop by creating simple, yet undeniably catchy grooves. Her bass parts often jump around in both register and methods of attack; she will frequently implement a single "pop" in the higher register to contrast the lower plucked notes. At times, she creates a groove that remains largely unchanged throughout long sections of the song, as evidenced by "Once In A Lifetime" and Tom Tom Club's "Won't Give You Up." This approach defined a style of bass playing and popular music of the 1980s—one that existed in the clubs of New York City well before hitting the mainstream. In doing so, it developed as the fusion of trance-inducing dance music and curiously creative counter-culture that broke at the crest of the new wave.

Where Can I Hear Her?
"Psycho Killer" Talking Heads, *Talking Heads 77*
Weymouth sets the stage for this song, standing alone with solid quarter notes that have made an indelible mark on popular music. The bass provides movement throughout the song by playing easily identifiable phrases, adding rhythmic variation, and offering a counterpoint line to the vocal melody of the bridge. Throughout the entirety of the song, each instrument adheres to a specific and repetitive part—single chords by the guitars and a simple drumbeat—with the bass providing the musical variation.

"Crosseyed and Painless"
Talking Heads, *Stop Making Sense*
During this trancy-dancy disco-reggae number, Weymouth holds down the groove during the introduction with a chill and syncopated line hinting at what is to come. As the band immediately jumps into the energetic and percussively driven song, the bass part focuses on simple notes with a leap in register. The breakdown features a revised part, with Weymouth leaving space and adding a high response to the call of single notes played by the keyboards.

"Genius Of Love" Tom Tom Club, *Tom Tom Club*
If you need to settle into a super catchy groove to play for the entirety of a song, this is a particularly good one. A reflection of popular music and early 1980s hip hop, it features a recurring

groove with varied melodies, vocal hooks, and short breaks where parts exit and re-enter the track. Fun fact: this song inspired Mariah Carey's smash hit, "Fantasy." While producers didn't sample the original Tom Tom Club recording, Weymouth and other members received writing credit for the song.

Krist Novoselic

"I dare you to learn this song. In fact, I double dare you to you learn this song!"

That's what the little voice inside my head said to me the first time I heard "Come As You Are" by Nirvana. I was a freshman in high school and had never touched a bass. As I sat on the floor of my friend's bedroom, listening to records in an attempt to make sense of our teenage angst and the world at large, this crazy voice told me I had to learn that song and, more specifically, I had to learn it on the bass. I very much dared myself to do it. The lick was hypnotic and melancholic, a repetitive beckoning for the listener to "come as you are" and embrace the sounds blasting from the speakers. While the name Krist Novoselic was, at that time, somewhat overshadowed by the entity known as Nirvana, his contributions to the world of rock are nothing short of legendary. His bass playing is energizing and authentic—simple when it needs to be, clever as it leads the listener through curious chord changes, and clearly designed to fit the attitude of the song. As a member of Nirvana and a multi-instrumentalist who continues to work with various bands, Novoselic is a bass player to know.

Who Is Krist Novoselic?

Born in 1965, Novoselic grew up in San Pedro, California as the eldest of three children to Croatian immigrants. As a teenager, his family moved to Aberdeen, Washington and Krist took an interest in hard rock and punk. While in high school, he met his younger brother's friend, Kurt Cobain, and the two began playing music together. Cobain and Novoselic went through a series of drummers as they recorded their first trio album, Bleach (1989) before being introduced to Dave Grohl in 1990. Shortly after Grohl joined the band, Nirvana landed a record deal with DGC Records and went to LA to record Nevermind at Sound City Studios. With the release of Nevermind in 1991 and the success of "Smells Like Teen Spirit," the band toured extensively and released two more records, Incesticide (1992) and In Utero (1993). Following the release of their MTV Unplugged session, they received a Grammy for "Best Alternative Music Performance," in addition to multiple MTV Music Awards. After Cobain's untimely death in 1994, Nirvana broke up and both Novoselic and Grohl moved on to other musical projects.

Since the mid-1990s, Novoselic has worked with a number of groups, including The No WTO Combo, Eyes Adrift, Flipper, and his current band, Giants In The Trees. He has maintained his relationship with Grohl, making guest appearances both live and in the studio with the Foo Fighters and working with Grohl and Sir Paul McCartney on the soundtrack to Sound City: Real to Reel. In addition to his musical endeavors, Krist has written numerous pieces for Seattle Weekly and has been politically active with the group JAMPAC (Joint Artists and Musicians Political Action Committee).

Let's Talk Style
It's safe to say that Novoselic deserves to be among the rock trio royalty, sitting confidently beside Jack Bruce and Mike Dirnt, Noel Redding and Geddy Lee, Lemmy and Sting. The trio setting is not for the faint of heart, rather it is for the players with attitude, attention to detail, and a clear understanding of the power of their notes.

Within the context of Nirvana, Novoselic is the heavy-handed, big-bottomed anchor that emphasizes Grohl's crash symbol, reinforces Cobain's chords, and induces hypnosis with steady bass lines. Master of the descending slide, he alerts the listener to transitions: verse to chorus, quiet moment to brutally aggressive musical outburst. His live tone is comparable to drinking a mug of ginger tea. It is comforting and warm, a respite from the cold, and surprisingly assertive with a bite that will hopefully do your body good. He obviously has something to say and does so with pick in hand and an overdriven amp. His style is felt as much as it is heard, with the decision of when or when not to play adding as much character and dynamic movement as the notes played.

Where Can I Hear Him?
"Smells Like Teen Spirit"
Nirvana, From The Muddy Banks of the Wishkah

Dropping in with a descending slide, Novoselic mimics the opening riff before settling into the beautifully repetitive progression of the verse. While creating the bed for Curbain's vocals and providing contrast to the high notes that ring out on guitar, the bass part locks in with Grohl's drums in a way that inspires head banging and the desire to rip holes in one's jeans. Throughout the solo section, he manages to bring even greater intensity to the stage, supporting the melody with enough sensitivity to take it down a notch for the final verse. This attention to dynamics and keen understanding of how to embrace and execute a part solidifies him as not just an accompanist, but as an equal third.

"Lithium" Nirvana, Nevermind

This song is a lesson in presence, dynamics, and arrangement. It cycles through every possibility of the bass performing within the context of a power trio: the bass sits out at first, entering at the chorus like a wrecking ball. It takes a subtle approach to the second verse, adding enough bottom to support the changes and adding an inversion to provide contrast. It becomes the driving force of the bridge, with heavy root notes and groovy fills serving as a counterpoint to Cobain's vocals. And finally, the third verse provides a moment of musical relief, with just the bass and drums backing up the vocals until the full band finishes out the song.

"Sliver" Nirvana, Incesticide

Novoselic opens the song with a perfect rock bass line: simple, grooving, and effortless. His performance is suddenly infused with adrenaline, the chorus opening up with heightened aggression and a significantly more overdriven tone. The two sections live in perfect contrast to one another, a subtle verse that tells a story and the angsty response of the chorus, a plea reinforced by amplification and attitude.

Mike Dirnt

The diverse landscape of rock music in the 1990s reflects the contrast between ethereal British bands, alternative and grunge stemming from the Seattle area, and the pop-punk renaissance that birthed bands such as Green Day, The Offspring, and Weezer. They inspired many teenagers to learn power chords on the electric guitar, dye their hair, and slam their bedroom door in an act of defiance. Bassist Mike Dirnt of Green Day stands out as an exceptional power-trio player with assertive bass lines, vocal harmonies, and an edgy, frosted-tip image to boot.

Who Is Mike Dirnt?
A California native, Michael Ryan Pritchard was born in 1972. His parents divorced while he was still young and his mother's financial troubles resulted in a difficult childhood. During middle school, he began playing guitar and became fast friends with Billie Joe Armstrong. The two started to play together, forming their first band Sweet Children in high school with drummer John Kiffmeyer

and bass player Sean Hughes. Mike began playing bass when Hughes decided to leave the band. He quickly adopted the nickname "Dirnt" when he found that plucking the unamplified strings on the instrument sounded to him like, "dirnt, dirnt, dirnt."

In 1989, the band changed their name to Green Day for the release of their first album *39/Smooth*. They went on tour the day Dirnt graduated from high school and drummer Tre Cool joined the band in late 1990. After the release of *Kerplunk*, the band signed with Reprise Records and have since released over a dozen live and studio recordings including *Dookie*, *Warning*, and *American Idiot*. Green Day has received five Grammy awards, adapted the record *American Idiot* into a Tony-nominated Broadway show, and has been inducted in to the Rock & Roll Hall of Fame.

Still an active member of Green Day, Mike Dirnt has recorded with various side projects, including The Frustrators, Foxboro Hot Tubs, Screeching Weasel, and Squirtgun. He has appeared in a variety of films and television series, such as *King Of The Hill*, *The Simpsons Movie*, and *Anchorman: The Legend Continues*.

Let's Talk Style

The power trios of every generation have in common a bass player who isn't afraid of the spotlight, or to assert their musical ability and personality. Dirnt's playing is the perfect combination of overdriven tone, showmanship, rhythmic finesse, and melodic hooks. He's a natural at knowing how to deal with space, whether it's a quick fill to usher in a new section of a song, pulsing eighth notes, or choosing to lay out during a drum or guitar break.

A handful of songs on the more recent Green Day records feature medley-style compositions that highlight the bass during transitions or introductions. Dirnt often sets the stage for the song, outlining the harmonic movement before the guitar enters. He frequently chooses simplicity and consistency over variation, a staple approach of the punk genre, though he isn't afraid of being captivating and complex when the time is right.

Dirnt's notion of dynamics stems as much from density as decibels; he often plays with register to assert dynamic energy by jumping up an octave. This tends to fill out the space, despite the fact that he may be playing the same rhythmic part. He effectively takes things up a notch by focusing on where the drummer accents the rhythm; he'll latch on to the crash hits to add emphasis to punches and give more power to the power trio.

Where Can I Hear Him?
"Longview" Green Day, *Dookie*
One of the breakthrough singles that put Green Day on the map, this tune opens with a descending muted slide into an iconic bass line. The song is played on an instrument tuned a half-step down; the low Db rings out and allows for Dirnt to play chords as part of

the bass line. Dirnt plays a variation of the main line during the first half of the second verse and, at the end of the song, a catchy and welcome reinterpretation of the original theme. Check out the raw-sounding hammer-ons fueling the chorus and the descending line that Dirnt plays to mimic the vocal melody of "motivation" during the bridge.

"Last Of The American Girls"
Green Day, *21st Century Breakdown*
There's nothing more perfect than driving eighth notes and Dirnt certainly does this technique justice. This song is pure pop-punk goodness, with simple I-IV-V changes, catchy lyrics, and a great-sounding overdriven bass tone. If you're new to pick playing, try practicing along with this song to develop good technique, tone, and rhythmic consistency.

"East Bay of Urden Bay"
The Frustrators, *Bored In The USA*
Mike Dirnt recorded two albums with this group, a band comprised of players from other established punk rock bands. "East Bay" features the bass on hyper-drive, with Dirnt's speedy, pick-driven groove in the forefront. Following a traditional blues progression, his line drives the song as mumbling vocals and screechy guitars battle one another. It's a great example of his gritty, in-your-face

tone and agile picking. The same could be said for "West of Texas," another album cut from this project.

Colin Greenwood

Longevity, innovation, and widespread influence are three characteristics that define legendary musicians and ensembles—Radiohead among them. This band has produced intricate and envelope-pushing music since the early 1990s by embracing technology and blending genres. Their beautifully composed, dynamic, and often trance-like creative expression is supported by the bass lines of Colin Greenwood. His careful execution puts "Everything In Its Right Place."

Who Is Colin Greenwood?
Colin Greenwood was introduced to music at a young age, thanks to his family members and the influence of his teachers. As a teenager, he attended the Abingdon School where, at the age of 12, he met future Radiohead vocalist Thom Yorke. Colin began studying classical guitar at the age of 15 and, after leaving Abingdon School, studied English at Cambridge University.

The early days of Radiohead began with Colin and Thom York's project On A Friday, formed in 1986. Ed O'Brien, Phil Selway, and Johnny Greenwood (Colin's younger brother) eventually joined the band and they began writing music and playing local shows. Inspired by old soul records and the necessity for low end in the newly formed group, Colin assumed the role of bass player. While working at a music store, Colin managed to get a demo into the hands of EMI representatives who eventually signed the band.

After changing their name to Radiohead, the band released their first single, "Creep," in 1992 and began their climb toward commercial success. Between the release of *Pablo Honey* in 1993 and *A Moon Shaped Pool* in 2016, Radiohead has received multiple nominations for BRIT awards, and three Grammy's for Best Alternative Music Album (*OK Computer, Amnesiac, In Rainbows*). Inducted into the Rock & Roll Hall of Fame in 2019, the band continues to record and tour. During any down time, Greenwood works on side projects and music for film.

Let's Talk Style
We all learn that patience is a virtue, and while this rings true in most aspects of life, it's particularly valuable in the world of music. Knowing *when* to play becomes as important as knowing *what* to play. Space, arrangement, and anticipation are the cornerstones of Radiohead's music—Greenwood's ability to play exactly the right

thing at the right time makes him an essential element of the band. Whether coming in with a bass line at the beginning of the song, entering halfway through, or remaining absent entirely, he is playing (or not playing) what is most appropriate for the composition. In doing so, the entrance of the bass becomes an important moment; it introduces a new theme that greatly enhances the density of the song while grabbing the attention of the listener.

Another attribute that Greenwood brings to Radiohead is his notion of bass as a *function* without the limitations of bass as an instrument. He's a multi-instrumentalist, sometimes picking up the upright bass, stepping behind the keyboard, or generating luscious sounds on a synth. This gives him the ability to develop textures and parts that fulfill the sonic spectrum of bass without necessarily playing a bass guitar. He maintains the bottom end by sticking to the lower frequencies but his synth and keyboard parts give him the opportunity to play with the envelope of the note. He manipulates the attack, sustain, and decay of the notes to create pads or unique sounding lines that may not work otherwise. When he does stick with the bass guitar, he adopts a similar approach and uses a variety of pedals to augment the sound of the instrument.

Where Can I Hear Him?

"Airbag" Radiohead, *OK Computer*

During the first half of this song, Greenwood's bass part is simple and sporadic, acting like tasty candied pecans scattered sparingly in a salad. This part is characterized by silence and restraint rather than continuity and drive. As the song continues, Greenwood adopts a more traditional and present approach. He toggles between just a few notes, further developing the theme introduced earlier in the song.

"Climbing Up The Walls" Radiohead, *OK Computer*

Greenwood puts the bass guitar down and steps behind the synth for this song, providing the perfect sonic backdrop for spacey guitars and atmospheric vocals. He still fulfills the role of the bass player, though the synth allows him to play with the envelope, character and sustain of the note. The tone evolves and blossoms with a rich and distorted texture instead of decaying as it would on a bass guitar. The part is simple yet the sound is complex.

"15 Step" Radiohead, *In Rainbows*

Although it takes awhile for the bass to make an appearance, it delivers a solid groove that complements the odd-meter of the song. Colored by fierce fills and an intricate descending line, the bass part weaves in and out, leaving plenty of space for reverb-drenched vocals, miscellaneous shouts, and percussive sounds.

Section III:

The Session Ace

Ray Brown

If you were to go digging through a bin of old jazz records, you would encounter the name Ray Brown. His prolific career as a sideman, composer, bandleader, and session bassist kept him working for over fifty years with artists that include Charlie Parker, Oscar Peterson, Ella Fitzgerald, Quincy Jones, and countless others. Whether you're aspiring to learn the fundamentals of jazz, expand your repertoire, or find inspiration as a soloist, Ray Brown is a bass player to know.

Who Is Ray Brown?
A native of Pittsburgh, Pennsylvania, Ray Brown grew up playing piano and made the transition to bass while in high school. He began his professional career playing in local jazz clubs and moved to New York City in 1945. Brown met a handful of jazz greats upon his arrival, including Dizzy Gillespie, who immediately hired him for both his big band and smaller ensembles. Within a few years, he became widely known throughout the jazz and bebop circuit in

New York, playing with Gillespie, Jazz at the Philharmonic, and Ella Fitzgerald. In addition to being Fitzgerald's accompanist, the two were married for a short period. In the early 1950s, Brown recorded and toured with the Modern Jazz Quartet and began a long stint with the Oscar Peterson Trio.

By the mid-1960s, he decided it was time to head to the West Coast. He settled in Los Angeles to focus on session work and television dates. There, he was frequently called upon to accompany Frank Sinatra, Nancy Wilson, Sarah Vaughn, Tony Bennett, and many others. In addition to performing, he produced shows for the Hollywood Bowl, managed the up-and-coming Quincy Jones, played cello, and eventually got to work with Duke Ellington. In later years, he recorded and toured with his own trio and focused on education, mentoring, and developing instructional books. Ray Brown passed away in his sleep after a round of golf on July 2, 2002, just prior to a scheduled performance in Indianapolis, Indiana.

Let's Talk Style

Ray Brown's credits read like an encyclopedic list of jazz heavyweights. His tone and musical approach embodied the fundamentals of the genre, making him an exemplary and essential study. Approaching harmony in a way that was accessible yet smart, he gracefully composed walking bass lines that incorporated chordal, scalar, and chromatic motion. He created counter-melodies that steered the song through the changes and, when it was time to groove, he was ready to throw down with funky, blues inspired embellishments.

From a rhythmic standpoint, Brown clearly held himself accountable for time-keeping and establishing the feel of the song. Whether he was playing a straight-ahead standard or a mild-mannered ballad, you would hear clear and confident quarter notes dictating the tempo and pocket. He inherently understood when and how to use pickup notes to shape the overall feel without being overly assertive. This mature and sophisticated approach to using percussive accents, dead notes, string raking, and short melodic phrases demonstrated his diverse rhythmic vocabulary and clearly painted him as the driving force of an ensemble.

With a keen ear for arrangement, much of his trio work features big-band style hits and well-executed rhythmic transitions. Brown frequently mimicked the phrasing of other band members in a call-and-response manner to establish conversational interplay and rhythmic variation. In doing so, he encouraged improvisation without losing the groove or overshadowing the soloist.

When it comes to tone, consider Ray Brown the benchmark for what an upright bass should sound like. His notes rang out clearly, confidently, and in tune. Difficult moves, such as jumping from one register to another or sliding up and down the neck were flawless due to his masterful technique. Runs that concluded with the robust attack of an open string managed to open up the music and provide just enough time to reposition on the fretboard.

Where Can I Hear Him?
"America The Beautiful" The Ray Brown Trio, *Walk On*

From the last recorded and released performance of the Ray Brown Trio, this song begins with a lighthearted bass introduction that sets the stage for the song. With a gentle piano accompaniment, Brown takes the melody, phrasing it as if he were a vocalist. The band enters with an energetic interpretation of the patriotic theme, with Brown walking through the changes using hefty quarter notes. As the drummer and pianist infuse other rhythmic elements, Brown remains the steady time-keeper until the end of the song, where they all hit together in a big-band fashion.

"Night Train" The Oscar Peterson Trio, *Night Train*

As the title track of the record, this tune is a quintessential example of how to walk through a mid-tempo bluesy shuffle. During the head of the tune, Brown joins in with a simple octave jump to accompany the keyboard part, adding fills during the breaks and punctuating the lines with the drummer. His solo explores the range of the instrument in a perfectly controlled manner. He slides between the blue notes of the scale, plays to the chords, and leaves himself space for embellishment while reiterating melodic themes.

"Sophisticated Lady"
Ray Brown and Duke Ellington, *This One's for Blanton*

This particular record is unique for a few reasons. First, Ray Brown had always wanted to work with Duke Ellington and this album proved to be the realization of that dream. Second, it features two of the most distinguished personalities in jazz conversing for all to hear. This piece begins with Brown's solo, complete with trills and slides that allude to the melody. They move through the changes together, with Brown providing the rhythmic foundation before dropping out for Ellington's solo. The song concludes with another solo from Brown, restating the original themes and acting as a bass-heavy bookend.

Red Callender

As a uniquely talented upright bassist and tuba player, Red Callender spent most of his career as an L.A. session cat. Within the jazz idiom, he can be heard on recordings by Louis Armstrong, Billie Holiday, Art Tatum, Charlie Parker, and many others. His open-minded attitude, musical sensitivity, and skillful nature as a multi-instrumentalist led to session calls with pop and rock artists including Sam Cooke, The Monkees, Ry Cooder, and James Taylor. If you happen to be browsing through album credits, you'll often find his name alongside fellow session bassists Leland Sklar and Willie Weeks, clearly indicating him as a bass player to know.

Who Is Red Callender?
Born in Haynesville, VA, George Sylvester "Red" Callender began studying music at a young age and immediately gravitated toward the tuba and upright bass. He moved to Los Angeles as a teenager and found himself recording with Louis Armstrong by the age of 19. This quickly led to more session opportunities as he landed gigs

with Billie Holiday, Bing Crosby, Earl Hines, Charlie Parker, Art Tatum, Erroll Garner, Nat King Cole, and other jazz heavy weights. Around 1940, Callender began teaching lessons to a determined young bass player named Charles Mingus.

From the 1940s to the 1960s, Callender continued to be a force to be reckoned with in the jazz world; he worked steadily as a sideman and put out numerous solo projects. Thanks to his versatility on the upright bass and tuba, as well as his professional demeanor, he was one of the first African-American musicians to regularly work in the L.A. session scene. By the 1970s, he began getting calls for blues, pop, and rock records with artists including Randy Newman, Rickie Lee Jones, and Gregg Allman. After a long and successful career, Callender passed away at the age of 76 due to thyroid cancer.

Let's Talk Style

To be a steadily working musician, it's important to have a diverse repertoire, an expansive knowledge of form and function, and the ability to listen and accompany other artists. Red Callender was a master of all three. His talent as a multi-instrumentalist brought melody to his bass playing, rhythmic sensibilities to the tuba, and beautiful tone to both.

As a bassist, he excelled at all forms of jazz ensemble playing; he appropriately asserted himself as the driving force of a trio, but could just as easily exercise traditionalism and restraint when playing with a big band. His walking lines combined chord arpeggios, diatonic melodic movement, and chromaticism to guide the band in an effortless manner. His ability to adapt to different styles of jazz is reflected by his rhythmic choices. He understands how to use long, steady notes to support a ballad, adhere to a staccato and tuba-like approach for New Orleans and Dixieland jazz, or provide brisk quarter notes to enhance the momentum of bebop.

Callender's talent as an arranger came through on his solo recordings, where he took a creative approach to standards by featuring the tuba as a lead instrument. He successfully paired it with higher woodwinds and French horn—a clever instrumentation that allowed for doubling of the melody and a distinctively orchestral air.

Where Can I Hear Him?
"Love For Sale"
Art Tatum, *Presenting the Art Tatum Trio*
Featured on many of Tatum's recordings, Callender exhibits taste, creativity, and expertise in this trio. Obviously aware of the movement of Tatum's left hand, Callender provides the perfect accompaniment to his piano playing. He switches back and forth between a root-5_{th} or root-root approach during the head of the tune and a walking bass line during the solo sections. His timing is

impeccable as he locks in with the drummer and further emphasizes the piano chords.

"Foggy Day" Red Callender, *Speak Low*

This particular record features Callender's original arrangements. He plays tuba exclusively as the lead instrument and is accompanied by bassist Red Mitchell. As Mitchell clearly and sophisticatedly walks through the changes, Callender focuses on melodic interplay. A surprising musical moment happens when the bass and tuba trade solos. Callender begins the conversation, a dialogue ensues, and the section concludes with a unison line. At the end of the song, a dissonant call and response between the bowed upright, tuba, and woodwind instruments mimics the sound of a train horn in the distance.

"Easy Money" Rickie Lee Jones, *Rickie Lee Jones*

Callender sets the tone for this song with his distinctive, hearty, and soulful bass playing. He effortlessly walks through the changes, punctuates the hits, and brings a "cool jazz" attitude with a New Orleans twist to complement Jones' intricate vocal phrasing. This record, as well as many others from the mid to late 1970s, features Callender on the upright bass and Willie Weeks on electric.

Joe Osborn

If you're familiar with "The Wrecking Crew," a group of musicians that dominated the L.A. recording scene in the 1960s and '70s, then you probably know that these players jumped from session to session, providing the sonic backdrop to popular culture, and racking up credit after credit on top-ten hits. Joe Osborn's tenure as part of the Crew resulted in an extremely successful recording career. With his brilliant melodic phrases and the groovy bass lines on records by Simon and Garfunkel, The Carpenters, The Mamas and The Papas, The 5_{th} Dimension, Glen Campbell, and Johnny Rivers, Joe Osborn is one of the quintessential bass players to know.

Who Is Joe Osborn?

Joe Osborn hails from Mound, Louisiana, though his musical journey began after moving to Shreveport. First playing guitar and then switching to bass, he spent a year working in Las Vegas before moving back to Shreveport. He was recommended to Ricky Nelson, joined his band, and moved to the West Coast to begin his career as a touring and session musician. During the early 1960s, he recorded his first number-one hit, Ricky Nelson's "Travelin' Man." Thanks to producer Lou Adler, he began getting calls alongside "Wrecking Crew" drummer Hal Blaine and keyboardist Larry Knechtel. Osborn quickly took to studio work, recording music for television and making records for artists like The Monkees, Neil Diamond, Kenny Rogers, The Partridge Family, Billy Joel, and many others.

Desiring a change of pace, he moved to Nashville in 1974 to continue his career as a session bassist. There, he racked up credits with Merle Haggard, Ricky Skaggs, Amy Grant, J.J. Cale, and Tanya Tucker, just to name a few. Years later, he decided to move back to Louisiana with his family and retired from playing bass. He passed away in 2018 at the age of 81.

Let's Talk Style
Joe Osborn was the kind of player you called when you needed something to sound good. It's as simple as that. His keen understanding of popular form, dynamics, and sonic density made him the perfect musical conversationalist. Like a good friend, he knew when to listen and when to speak, when to chime in with a short word of encouragement or when to showcase his wisdom with an insightful monologue. Osborn was able to wait tacitly through sparse sections that highlight the lyrics and melody and recognize when to take an assertive role with a crafty and well-executed bass

line. He knew when to offer a different point of view by playing a 3_{rd} or 5_{th} instead of the root note and when to reiterate a point by doubling a theme or melodic phrase.

An Osborn "signature" is quick root-5_{th} movement—rather than outlining the triad, he omits the 3_{rd} and briskly toggles between just the two notes. This bouncy rhythm drives the band while remaining true to the classic sense of low-end harmony. Another signature move involved playing a I-IV chord progression: he frequently played the major 3_{rd} ascending through the progression (providing a half step leading tone before hitting the IV chord) and a minor 3_{rd} descending from the IV to the I (this highlights the $b7_{th}$ of the IV chord). One last example: Playing his 1961 Fender Jazz bass, he created a fine balance between the bright attack of a pick with the dark sound of rarely-changed flatwound strings—it magically sits in the mix and sounds just right.

Where Can I Hear Him?
"Never My Love" The Association, *Insight Out*
Mimicking the opening theme, Osborn favors the half-step leading tones to draw the listener from chord to chord during the verses. He adheres to a diatonic approach during the chorus, following the major scale as he moves through the progression. Infusing the bridge with momentum, his signature rapid root-5_{th} movement counteracts the lush and airy vocal line.

"Keep The Customer Satisfied"
Simon and Garfunkel, *Bridge Over Troubled Water*

Osborn brings an energetic, blues-inspired bass line to this deep cut, a welcome juxtaposition to the ballads that bookend the record. A tutorial in unusual blues progression playing, he shuffles with strong root notes and 5_{th}-6_{th} fills. He opens up during the choruses with a busier, major pentatonic approach that mimics the vocal "ohs." Ending in a climactic, horn-driven outro, Osborn adds more color by highlighting the octave and cleverly walking through the chords.

"Close To You" The Carpenters, *Close To You*

Playing with a gentle and sensitive hand, Osborn takes a minimalist approach to the bass line. He relies mostly on the root and 5_{th}, playing with exactly the right note duration to glue together the simple drum groove. He also sneaks in short melodic phrases, such as the high descending line during the verse following the bridge. Getting a bit more creative during the outro of the song, he adds slight variation with simple, staccato arpeggios and melodic fills emphasizing the up-beats.

Bernard Edwards

You've heard his bass lines at weddings, on the radio, at the supermarket, and even while waiting on the phone for the next available representative. His grooves defined the funk and disco era with their syncopated and infectious hooks, in-your-face tone, and get-your-booty-on-the-dance-floor swagger. And, as if they weren't iconic enough, early producers of hip-hop decided his bass lines would provide the perfect backdrop to this new musical and cultural phenomenon brewing across America. Bernard Edwards is the funk master who teamed up with Nile Rodgers in the 1970s to form Chic and to produce records for other chart-topping artists such as Diana Ross and Sister Sledge. In addition to solo records and a long list of songwriting credits, he has provided the low end for recordings by David Bowie, Madonna, Robert Palmer, Rod Stewart, and many more.

Who Is Bernard Edwards?

Bernard Edwards was born in Greenville, North Carolina in 1952 and spent most of his early years in Brooklyn. He cut his teeth in the New York music scene during the late 1960s and by his late teens, was the musical director and bass player in the Big Apple Band. Nile Rodgers fortuitously joined the band and the two struck up a partnership that later morphed into their own group—Chic. They signed with Atlantic Records and were nominated for a Grammy in 1977 thanks to the song "Dance, Dance, Dance." In the next two years, they released *C'est Chic* with the dance-floor classic "Le Freak," and the mega hit "Good Times" on 1979's *Risqué*. All the while, Edwards and Rodgers wrote and produced hit songs for other artists including "We Are Family" by Sister Sledge and the Diana Ross singles "Upside Down" and "I'm Coming Out."

During the late 1970s, hip-hop was in its infancy until the success of "Rapper's Delight" by The Sugarhill Gang brought it to maturity. This song, which featured Edwards' bass line, quickly became a mainstream musical phenomenon and paved the way for sampling in rap, hip-hop, and R&B. Since then, countless Edwards/Rodgers productions have been adapted to provide the musical background for hits by Salt-N-Pepa, Notorious B.I.G., Will Smith, and many others.

In the meantime, Edwards and Rodgers continued to release music and tour as Chic until 1983, at which time they decided to pursue other projects. Edwards then recorded a solo record and formed The Power Station with Robert Palmer, Duran Duran's Andy Taylor and Chic's drummer Tony Thompson. Still an in-demand session bassist, he played on records by Paul Simon, Mick Jagger, Joe Cocker, and Rod Stewart, as well as on Nile Rodgers-produced projects, including David Bowie's *Let's Dance* and Madonna's *Like A Virgin*. After a long hiatus, Chic reunited in 1992 with the release of *Chic-ism*. Following a run of performances in Japan in 1996, Bernard Edwards passed away at the age of 43 due to complications with pneumonia.

Let's Talk Style

Bernard Edwards was a master of taste. A player with great technical ability, he exercised restraint and control in the most musical way—creating a part and letting it guide the song. His lines are simple enough that you can sing along to them, yet seem fresh over and over again due to the subtle tension they create. He defined what we consider a "bass groove"—a hook that doesn't need elaboration to be interesting, and in fact, is more effective when executed correctly over and over again.

When it comes to being a great rhythm player, it all comes down to the plucking hand's ability to control precision, articulation, and note duration. Edwards was keenly aware of this and utilized different plucking-hand techniques (fingerstyle playing, slapping, or using a pick) without compromising the pocket or authenticity of the groove. While most players have a tendency to use slap bass as a means to showcase their technical facility, he used the slap and pop attack as a means of adding character to the note. It contributes to the sound and feel of the part and doesn't feature gratuitous technical chops. This approach differentiates him from other slap players of the day and upcoming eras, affirming his sense of taste and musicality.

Where Can I Hear Him?
"Good Times" Chic, *Risqué*
Written and produced by Bernard Edwards and Nile Rodgers, this has become one of the most iconic, genre-defying, and influential grooves in the history of recorded music. The song originally hit the top of the charts with Chic in 1979, but the record (and Edwards' bass line) quickly expanded beyond the world of disco and funk into hip-hop when The Sugarhill Gang used it as the basis for "Rapper's Delight." This helped ignite the flame of a new musical genre and "Good Times" went on to be sampled or referenced in countless other recordings. The iconic three-note phrase that begins the groove also inspired "Another One Bites The Dust" by Queen, released the following year. In other words, most of the people on planet Earth have heard some version of this bass line.

"Material Girl" Madonna, *Like A Virgin*

A beautiful portrait of perfect pop production, this song exemplifies Edwards' clear tone, punchy articulation, and attention to note duration. He executes a specific and clearly defined part that provides the rhythmic foundation while leaving space for the rest of the ensemble. This style of production mimics that of many Chic records, where the bass plays a simple yet effective part that rarely varies and is instead catchy and repetitive. He takes a slightly busier approach to the choruses by accenting the higher octaves and nodding to the disco grooves of the era; this sense of motion creates greater tension gracefully relieved when he returns to the original pattern.

"Glad To Be Here" Bernard Edwards, *Glad To Be Here*

Featuring a ridiculously funky slap bass groove, this solo project by Edwards is a rare find in the vinyl bin. A showcase for his overall musicality, Edwards exercises precision, restraint, and taste in the way he plays. The song is built around a syncopated bass groove that provides the musical hook to the choruses and intertwines with the drums and rhythm guitar. He takes a simpler approach to the verses that draws listeners' attention to the vocals and leaves room for the part to grow dynamically in other sections of the song.

Louis Johnson

Have you ever wanted to "slappa da bass?" If so, you'll need to channel your inner Louis Johnson, bust out your own thunder thumbs, and inspire people to get down on the dance floor. Whether you're listening to hits by Michael Jackson, Michael McDonald, or The Brothers Johnson, you can't help but be inspired by his creative, articulate, and downright funky bass playing.

Who Is Louis Johnson?
Born in 1955, Louis Johnson appeared on the Los Angeles music scene as a professional bass player in the 1970s. Alongside his brother George, the two played with Bobby Womack and The Supremes before joining Billy Preston's band in 1972. After working with Preston on *Music In My Life* and *The Kids and Me,* the brothers left the band and ended up working with producer Quincy Jones on his project, *Mellow Madness.* This led to a unique partnership with Jones, as he started producing The Brothers

Johnson's records, beginning with *Look Out for #1*. The following releases, *Right On Time*, *Blam!!*, and *Light Up The Night*, all faired well on the Billboard charts by featuring funk and disco grooves with a heavy emphasis on Louis' slap playing.

In addition to working with The Brothers Johnson, Louis was an in-demand session player throughout the 1980s. Quincy Jones enlisted him to play on Michael Jackson's *Thriller* and *Off The Wall*—his beautifully infectious bass playing on "Billie Jean" is reason enough for him to be a bass player to know. Johnson also worked with Herbie Hancock, Bill Withers, Grover Washington, Jr., Lee Ritenour, Herb Alpert, Aretha Franklin, George Benson, Michael McDonald, and fellow funk master, Stanley Clarke. Some of his iconic bass lines, including Michael McDonald's "I Keep Forgettin' (Every Time You're Near)" have been sampled on rap, hip-hop, and R&B hits. His nickname, "Thunder Thumbs," has been rightfully earned due to his early adoption of slap bass and the aggressive tone of Leo Fender's Music Man Stingray. Johnson passed away in 2015.

Let's Talk Style

Johnson was one of the true grandfathers of funk and slap bass playing. On a par with the likes of Larry Graham, he played with a diverse and evolving technical style. Favoring the aggressive tone of his thumb and index finger, his mastery of this punchy and percussive technique is evident throughout his body of work.

As one of the early adopters of slapping, Johnson approached rhythm from both the right and left hand. His plucking-hand technique varied throughout the years, often due to various hand issues to which he was forced to adapt. If you get the opportunity to look at his videos, you'll see that he had an equally forceful and defined attack with his thumb striking the top of the string or pulling from below. Similarly, he used his index finger to pull (or pop) the string, and at times, grabbed the string simultaneously with his thumb for extra snap.

His fretting hand was equally important as a percussive tool. By integrating dead notes, chokes, hammer-ons, pull-offs, and slides, he brought greater sophistication and complexity to slap licks. He instinctually created syncopated patterns with both hands and took a playful approach to rhythmic variation.

When it came to different slap patterns, Johnson played to the advantages of the instrument and most importantly, to the key of the song. Playing in E or A yields the luxury of using open strings and anchoring around the pentatonic notes in the middle of the neck (the 5_{th}-9_{th} frets). Johnson also had the physical advantage of being able to reach his left thumb over the top of the neck to fret notes on the E string. This gave him the flexibility to transpose certain slap patterns to other keys by providing the fretted root note on the E string. His patterns typically revolved around the minor pentatonic box, relying heavily on the 3_{rd}, 5_{th}, and $b7_{th}$ scale degrees. Many of his basslines also feature the now-common slap pattern, root-octave-root, played up and down the neck with a triplet rhythmic figure.

Where Can I Hear Him?
"Strawberry Letter 23"
The Brothers Johnson, *Right On Time*
Warning: if you listen to this song, you will probably find yourself crinkling your nose and sporting the "stank face." Featuring a few different slap parts, Johnson creates a complex groove with edgy pops, double attacks on the lower strings, ascending octaves, and a chromatic triplet line.

"Get On The Floor" Michael Jackson, *Off The Wall*
As one of Quincy Jones' preferred bass players, Johnson contributed some superbly funky bass parts to both *Thriller* and *Off The Wall*. Co-written with Michael Jackson, this tune is unmistakably Louis. A prominent and aggressive slap tone gives the song a funky, dance-floor feel. He integrates heavily punctuated pops, slides into notes, accents with the higher octave, and an abundance of percussive attacks.

"Stomp" The Brothers Johnson, *Light Up The Night*
The tune begins with a simmering, percussive groove that nods to the chorus and features layered rhythm guitar parts, strings, and horns. Jumping into the verse, Johnson gets the feet a-movin' with

a staccato, two-phrase bass line built around the root and b7th. During the choruses, he settles into a syncopated groove that follows the minor scale, descending and then ascending, with back and forth step-wise motion guiding the line. As if these parts weren't enough to justify the cool factor of this song, Johnson busts out a super stanky slap breakdown.

Willie Weeks

Time and time again, I must pay homage to the movie that sparked the flame of my musical obsession, one that introduced me to a style with more passion and groove than any I had experienced, with an eclectic history that has influenced every genre of American music. Thank you, *Blues Brothers 2000*. While some may say this sequel to *The Blues Brothers* is a bit cheeky, it features many of the musical icons from the original and more. The final scene involves a battle between the Blues Brothers and the Louisiana Gator Boys, a band of all-stars who have made significant contributions to blues, R&B and country.

Fronted by B.B. King and Eric Clapton, the band is rounded out by Isaac Hayes, Billy Preston, Jimmie Vaughan, Travis Tritt, Koko Taylor, Bo Diddley, Grover Washington, Jr., and Steve Winwood. The rhythm section of Jack DeJohnette on drums and Willie Weeks on bass is second to none—these players have had as much influence on popular music as the artists they support. If you've never taken the time to explore the diverse and eclectic catalogue of Willie Weeks, then get ready to listen to a lot more records.

Who Is Willie Weeks?

Born in Salemburg, North Carolina, Weeks took up the bass in the early 1960s. Inspired by popular music, jazz, and the styles of James Jamerson, Ray Brown, and Ron Carter, he developed a musical style that is soulful, playful, and musically appropriate. By the early 1970s, he was doing sessions and gigs, including the famous 1972 live performance with Donny Hathaway at The Bitter End in New York. The rest of the '70s was marked by sessions on both upright and electric with David Bowie, George Harrison, Randy Newman, Stevie Wonder, James Taylor, The Rolling Stones, Ron Wood, and Rod Stewart. The following decades solidified him as a session great, featuring him on records by The Doobie Brothers, Michael McDonald, Rosanne Cash, Vince Gill, Etta James, Jimmy Buffett, John Mellencamp, Boz Scaggs, and John Mayer.

In addition to studio work, Weeks has an impressive live resume, touring with notable artists such as The Doobie Brothers, Steve Winwood, and Eric Clapton. He has been inducted into the North Carolina Music Hall of Fame and has appeared in the movies *Blues Brothers 2000* and *Lightning In A Bottle*. He continues to be an active session player with more recent credits including Mark Ronson, Keb' Mo', Wynonna Judd, and Buddy Guy.

Let's Talk Style

Whether you're into deep cuts or pop radio, you've probably heard Willie Weeks' bass lines. His ability to act as a musical chameleon has landed him session work of all genres, though he is most often featured on pop, blues, soul, and R&B records. He knows how to play with absolute attention to a part and when to add flare and personality. This mindfulness is the mark of a true professional.

In either situation, Weeks is a groove machine. His timing is exquisite, as is the placement and duration of his notes. He is the glue of a rhythm section—he knows when to lay back and play on the far end of the beat or when to groove slightly on top to give the band more momentum. A master of the "double hit," he often adds swing to a song with two attacks of the same note ("one-and" or "and-one"). This establishes a rhythmic skeleton to match the kick drum pattern and leaves room to play creatively over the rest of the bar. Alluding to his Jamersonian nature, he combines dead notes and string rakes with clever harmonic movement and excellent tone.

Where Can I Hear Him?
"Voices Inside (Everything Is Everything)"
Donny Hathaway, *Live (at The Bitter End, 1972)*
Cited as one of Weeks' greatest performances, this record captures the energy and authenticity of a live gig. His funky, punctuated notes establish a relentless groove that morphs throughout the song to

support the vocals and soloists, only to give way to an extended bass solo. Beginning with an elaboration of the original groove, he patiently introduces new rhythmic and melodic themes without ever dropping the time. Playing through the instrument's range, he executes high notes and chords supported by the low root. The solo is captivating and accessible to the listener, showcasing Weeks' skills as an instrumentalist without being overly indulgent.

"Unchain My Heart, Part 1"
John Scofield, *That's What I Say*

This record re-imagines Ray Charles' classics with the help of Willie Weeks and Steve Jordan. Weeks' slinky yet clearly defined playing respects the initial groove with just the right amount of improvisation to act as low-end ear candy. His chromatic double-attack line during the "B" section is nothing short of stanky, complete with quick octave hits, descending rakes, and slyly placed high accents. Check out the extended "part 2" for even more excellence.

"Takin' It To The Streets"
The Doobie Brothers, *Farewell Tour, 1983*

Weeks brings his punchy tone and expert articulation to this live performance, spearheading the song with a funky octave intro. He's the bass player anyone would want in their band—he plays to the songs' arrangement with both discipline and personality, executing each note perfectly yet adding groove and flavor that is uniquely his own.

Michael Rhodes

When I first moved to Nashville, a town with quite the reputation for musical excellence, I quickly learned that while Broadway was home to the Honky Tonks, plenty of good music was played off the beaten path. A few bass player buddies mentioned some cats to check out and, by no coincidence, the name Michael Rhodes came up time and time again. Who is this mysterious Michael Rhodes? Apparently, he has enough recording credits to rival (and perhaps surpass) Chuck Rainey and Leland Sklar. Could I really go to the Bluebird Cafe for $10 on a Monday night and hear him throw down on some blues? I went, I heard, and I returned home to practice. If you've never had a reason to check out Michael Rhodes, you do now.

Who Is Michael Rhodes?
Hailing from Monroe, LA, Michael Rhodes took to music at an early age, playing guitar and later picking up the bass. Before settling in Nashville, Rhodes spent time in Austin and Memphis, working

with Alan Rich. His move to Nashville in the 1970s resulted in session work for publishing companies and major label artists. As country music began to boom, so did Rhodes' career as a session player. He established himself as a first-call bassist, playing on records by Reba McEntire, Hank Williams, Jr., Rosanne Cash, Vince Gill, Faith Hill, Toby Keith, and Kenny Chesney, among others. With an intuitive feel for blues and soul music, Rhodes' resume also includes countless artists outside the realm of country, including Larry Carlton, Aaron Neville, Joan Osborne, and Joe Bonamassa.

Three decades later, Rhodes continues to be an active member of Nashville's musical community, anchoring records by Lady Antebellum, The Band Perry, Darius Rucker, and countless others. He often tours with Bonamassa and can be spotted playing around town with various side projects including The Fortunate Sons, The Players, and The World Famous Headliners. A recipient of the Academy of Country Music's Bass Player Of The Year award, his influence on Nashville's recording industry is second to none.

Let's Talk Style

As I sift through the mountains of records Michael Rhodes has played on, I find myself thinking that every track is perfect. The grooves are spot on, the choices of when to play or lay out create subtle dynamic changes, and the melodic lines cleverly lead the entire band. His innate understanding of note duration is unrivaled; his whole notes breathe and resonate with the track while his eighth notes create a bed of momentum that seems almost mechanically perfect, yet undeniably human. His vocabulary of feels, from traditional country and blues to modern pop, soul, and jazz, is not only varied, but characterized by authentic execution.

While Rhodes certainly has chops, most of the mainstream records he plays on require the "less is more" philosophy. His constant musical innovation over common chord progressions continues to justify his reputation as a player. He skillfully integrates chord inversions, reaching for melodic lines that move from 3_{rd} to 5_{th} rather than root to root. His knack for sneaking in high 5_{th} or dominant 7_{th} chords is uncanny, as is the phrasing and placement of many of his fills. While his approach is often varied and surprising, its internal logic means it rarely catches the listener off guard—he is enhancing instead of overplaying. He exudes the confidence of a master, the extensive lexicon of a musical linguist, and the humility that comes from recognizing the power of a song.

Where Can I Hear Him?
"Make A Liar Out Of Me" Striking Matches, *Nothing But The Silence*
There aren't many players who can bring a fresh musical approach to a familiar chord progression. Thankfully, Rhodes can and does with this song. Harmonically alluding to "All Along The

Watchtower," Rhodes creates a specific bass line relying on a high jump to the 10$_{th}$ of the chord and descending arpeggios that cleverly outline the rest of the progression. He retreats to beautifully simple root notes during the verse and elevates the chorus with a slightly busier, yet undeniably natural rhythmic approach. The song breaks down into a sparse chorus with Rhodes' high melodic backdrop, only to fall with grace and build into the final chorus, original theme, and solo outro.

"Spoonful" Joe Bonamassa, *Muddy Wolf at Red Rocks*
Rhodes lays down a slow and gritty groove on this classic blues tune, playing notes that seem to sink the listener into the song. He creates a foundation as comfortable as an old living room couch, yet he puts you on the edge of your seat as he jumps up the octave and pedals with intensity during the solo sections. His use of dynamics is intuitive—he knows exactly when to dig in, when to retreat with a muted tone, when to drop out, and when to usher in the rest of the band.

"The Rhythm Of The Pouring Rain"
Vince Gill, *These Days*
This 4-disc box set heavily features Rhodes on bass. He plays with supportive subtlety to enhance the lyrically driven songs and adds confident animation to the rocking numbers. "Rhythm" showcases his beautifully appropriate instincts as he elegantly follows the

chords while adding his signature high-register accents as lovely ear candy.

Sean Hurley

There's a lot to be said for bass players who know how to play a song. While it may seem like a simple thing, it takes a mature attitude and a keen ear to do so. Sure, soloing is fun, but slap technique and overly-assertive runs don't necessarily lead to being a working bass player. It's easy to get caught playing too many notes, compromising the groove, or stepping out at an inappropriate moment. If you ever need a reminder of how to best serve a song, I suggest you listen to a bass player who is superbly talented in this regard—Sean Hurley. A longtime member of Vertical Horizon, Hurley has also made an indelible mark on the L.A session scene.

Who Is Sean Hurley?
Hailing from Pittsfield, Massachusetts, Hurley's musical education began with saxophone during elementary school, quickly followed by bass. During his exposure to rock, classic R&B, and Motown, he developed both his ear and his reading chops. By the age of 16, Hurley was teaching lessons at a local music store and landed a

tour—first in a group supporting Arlo Guthrie and shortly thereafter as Guthrie's sideman. Following this early introduction to the touring lifestyle, he briefly attended Berklee College of Music before becoming a full-time player. While playing various shows and living in Boston, he auditioned for Vertical Horizon, landed the gig, and started recording and touring with the band.

In 2000, Hurley moved to L.A. to establish himself in the session scene. While he continued working with Vertical Horizon, he also wrote and recorded with Robin Thicke. This relationship served as a gateway for working with different producers and Hurley quickly racked up credits with Josh Groban, Annie Lennox, Alicia Keys, and Ringo Starr. After a few chance run-ins with John Mayer, he became his touring bassist and recorded Mayer's *Born and Raised* and *Paradise Valley*. More recently, he continues to be an active member of the L.A. scene and has credits with Alanis Morrissette, Melissa Ethridge, Michael Buble, Frankie Ballard, Idina Menzel, Colbie Caillat, and the late Leonard Cohen.

Let's Talk Style
Three words that describe Sean Hurley's playing are feel, intent, and class. As a session player, he has a deep understanding of groove and how to adapt to the feel of a song. He recognizes the subtle differences between playing a quarter note that punches or drives, one that is soulful and relaxed, or one that seems slightly

ahead of or behind the beat. Hurley can sink into the groove of the track as easily as he can be the one to define it.

As with all of the session greats, Hurley plays with intent. He obviously wants to make the song the best it can be for the artist and producer, satisfying his desire for perfection, while mixing in a bit of personality and some surprise. Each note is played in the right place, at the right time, and with the right attack. He can be reserved and supportive by playing simple parts that gracefully elevate a section of a song. Just as easily, he can play with a busier and aggressive attitude to drive a verse or open up a chorus.

Lastly, class. When you listen to a recording that he's played on, you realize he's taken a refined, dignified, and thoughtful approach. Like a chef knowing only a few ingredients are necessary to make a simple, elegant, and delicious dish, Hurley knows how to create a bass part with clean notes, warm tone, and respect for the song.

Where Can I Hear Him?
"Everything You Want"
Vertical Horizon, *Everything You Want*
The late 1990s produced an incredible number of hard-hitting, perfectly crafted pop-rock hits and this song is a good example. Hurley takes a punchy, rhythmically engaging approach to the verses—he grooves on the root with a clean and distinctive part. During the choruses, he opens up by playing notes of longer

duration to provide the perfect backdrop to the vocal melody. He effectively bumps up the energy during the bridge by pedaling through the chords and drops out with the rest of the band before the final verse. His parts are simple, musical, and exactly what the doctor ordered.

"Wildfire" John Mayer, *Paradise Valley*

Entering the song with a slide to the middle register, Hurley provides a warm and grooving accompaniment to the percussion and handclaps that drive the verses. The song picks up as he plays authoritative quarter notes to support the band, often interspersing classic R&B fills that highlight the 5_{th} and 6_{th} of the chord. Throughout the guitar solo and ride out of the song, he lets loose with chromatic fills and clever rhythmic interplay.

"Smithereens"
Annie Lennox, *Songs Of Mass Destruction*

This song is the perfect juxtaposition between mild-mannered chords and passionate, full-steam-ahead rock. With 10_{th} chords à la "Walk On The Wild Side," Hurley fills out the first verse and establishes the melancholy mood of the song. As the drums kick in, he matches the band's intensity and marries the kick drum pattern. He moves around the fretboard with ease, often sliding into the higher register or adding simple fills that provide just the right amount of energy.

Section IV:

The Eclectic

Richard Davis

As a college student, I spent many afternoons roaming the streets of New York City, constantly finding new routes to take me from my hole-in-the-wall apartment to the halls of academia. In an effort to create the ultimate soundtrack for my walks, I developed a healthy obsession with songwriters such as Van Morrison, Janis Ian, and Paul Simon, while supplementing the playlist with local jazz cats. Unbeknownst to me at the time, the same bass player appeared on some of my favorite walking music. With a list of album credits a mile long, ranging from jazz to pop and classical to rock, the incomparable Richard Davis is a bass player to know.

Who Is Richard Davis?
Hailing from Chicago, Richard Davis was born in 1930 and while growing up in a musical household, was inspired to pick up the double bass. Under high school band director Captain Walter Dyett, he learned traditional upright technique and music theory before attending Vandercook College. After a few years of working

in dance bands, he moved to New York City at the age of 24 and began to establish roots in the jazz scene. Davis soon joined Sarah Vaughan's touring and recording group while making a name for himself in the session world.

Between the late 1950s and mid-1970s, Davis played in and around New York City; he was an in-demand upright player for sessions, local gigs, and tours. His background in jazz established him as first-call for legendary artists like Kenny Burrell, Eric Dolphy, Pat Martino, Wes Montgomery, Elvin Jones, Stan Getz, Laura Nyro, Joe Zawinul, Miles Davis, and countless others. Furthermore, his classical technique translated to working with many of the top orchestras and conductors, including Leonard Bernstein and the New York Philharmonic, Igor Stravinsky, Pierre Boulez, and George Szell. With such eclectic musical roots and an inherently melodic approach, Davis also fielded calls for pop, rock, and songwriter sessions, most notably *Astral Weeks* by Van Morrison and records with Janis Ian, Bruce Springsteen, Barbara Streisand, Paul Simon, and Frank Sinatra.

In 1977, Davis decided to leave New York in favor of a teaching position at the University of Wisconsin at Madison. He has since received a number of honorary degrees and special achievement awards, including the National Endowment for the Arts Jazz Masters Award in 2014. He has been a dedicated faculty member for European Classical and Jazz bass studies and, in 1993, founded the Richard Davis Foundation for Young Bassists. An advocate for educational and cultural diversity, Davis continues to work with students and committees at the University to promote racial and ethnic awareness.

Let's Talk Style

With a background in classical music and jazz, Davis maintains a beautiful balancing act, shifting comfortably between a free-spirited improviser and a disciplined accompanist. He easily adapts his playing style to the session yet always maintains his own sound. Davis evidences a reverence for structure as he supports the song. He maintains a deep understanding of the classical tradition and demonstrates an approach to jazz that is both conventional and whimsical. His attitude and tone mirror each other as strong willed, charismatic, quirky, and full of heart.

As an accompanist, Davis has a keen understanding of playing *to* and *with* the song. Alongside singer-songwriters, he frequently acts as the primary time keeper and establishes forward motion alongside light percussion or a minimal drum kit. He fulfills a similar role on many jazz records, clearly keeping time with a strong walking bass line or groove. Without compromising the pocket, Davis cleverly intersperses unique fills, triplet-driven lines, and up-beat embellishments.

A particularly identifiable trait of Davis' playing is his use of range. Rather than adhering to the lower notes of the instrument, he frequently jumps back and forth, relying heavily on open strings as he moves up and down the neck, leaping to the higher register for fills and melodic lines. He often relies on long, descending glissandos to draw the listener from one note to the next and to fill the sonic space as a vocalist would.

Where Can I Hear Him?
"Summertime" Elvin Jones, *Heavy Sounds*
Opening with a haunting and powerfully bowed rendition of the melody, Davis explores the range and tonalities of the upright bass. His takes his time with the melody by using an intense vibrato to accent the notes. Upon switching to fingerstyle playing, he again plays to the melodic theme but branches out by incorporating other tonal colors. He integrates quick flourishes, moments of sonic experimentation, and descending slides. Following the drum solo, he returns to the melody with careful and majestic bowing. The song concludes with an edgy and contemporary exploration of the instrument that alludes to the title of the album.

"Astral Weeks" Van Morrison, *Astral Weeks*
If there's one instrument that propels this dynamic odyssey, it's Davis' upright bass. Firmly dictating the feel of the song, Davis plays a simple yet lively part that jumps between the two chords. He takes full advantage of the range of the instrument by jumping up the octave, playing the pattern in reverse, and by adding quick fills in the higher register. Midway through the track, he cleverly stays on

the root as the guitar chords continue to change; this adds harmonic diversity to a simple and repetitive progression. As the song comes to a close, he simplifies the pattern; taking his cue from Morrison's vocals. He subtly settles into long root notes and a series of light chords before having the final say with a bowed note.

"At Seventeen" Janis Ian, *Between The Lines*

Enhancing the nostalgia of Ian's lyrics, Davis' bass line carries the song with a dignified feel, eloquent voice leading, and a developing theme. Throughout the course of the song, he plays with obvious consideration for arrangement, beginning with a minimal approach and building dynamically through the verses. During pensive moments of the song, he retreats along with the rest of the rhythm section to draw attention to the prose. He uses long, descending slides to engender movement, provides counterpoint to the vocal melody, and adds syncopated fills in the higher register.

Bob Daisley

When I'm driving down the highway and Ozzy Osbourne's "Crazy Train" comes on the radio, it becomes difficult to adhere to the speed limit. The raw power of rock tempts me to put the pedal to the metal. I'd personally like to thank Bob Daisley for his contributions to that record and many others. His command of the instrument, eclectic musical background, and diverse resume makes him a bass player to know.

Who Is Bob Daisley?

A native of Sydney, Australia, Bob Daisley began his musical journey as a guitarist-turned-bassist at the age of 14. Inspired by soul music and the British Invasion, his first studio project was *Wide Open* with the Australian band Kahvas Jute. Quickly realizing that better musical opportunities lay elsewhere, he moved to London in 1970. Within a few years, he found himself touring and recording with Chicken Shack, Mungo Jerry, and Widowmaker. By the late '70s, he had joined Rainbow alongside Ronnie James Dio and

Ritchie Blackmore for several tours and an album, *Long Live Rock'n'Roll*. In 1979, Daisley had a chance meeting with Ozzy Osbourne at a bar in London. Shortly thereafter, he began recording Osbourne's debut solo record, *Blizzard of Ozz*.

The 1980s proved to be a busy decade for Daisley, as he bounced between a handful of successful projects. In addition to working with Ozzy Osbourne on his solo project, he recorded with Black Sabbath, Uriah Heep, and Yngwie Malmsteen. He had an "on again off again" touring relationship with these artists despite playing on many of their records. Daisley also established what would become a longtime association with Gary Moore, playing on several records and tours between the 1980s and mid-2000s. After returning to Australia in the early 2000s, he continued to write, record, and tour with various artists. He has published an autobiography, *For Facts Sake,* has a signature "Black Beauty" bass by Utopia Custom Shop, and remains an active member of the musical community.

Let's Talk Style

As with many of our Bass Players To Know, Daisley has the ability to jump from one musical scenario to another on account of his versatility as a player. He brings his signature tone and attitude to every project while contributing to the vision established by the artist. This is no doubt one of the reasons he gets called back for sessions and tours. Fretless bass? Sure. Pick? Absolutely.

Aggressive and busy in one song and mellow in the next? No problem.

Rooted in rock and blues, he holds down the groove with his mastery of the quarter note—listen to how he plays with an assertive attack and acute note duration to clearly define the feel. Both a pick and fingerstyle player, he excels at playing quick sixteenth notes, triplets, gallops, and cross string jumps; his integration of these varied techniques influenced countless rock and metal records of the 1980s.

Daisley's thorough knowledge of theory is evident in both the riffs he creates and his sparse, melodic movement when playing fretless on Gary Moore records. Often implementing scale-based fills or lines, he takes a creative approach by moving in different directions, for example, playing a few notes ascending, then descending, then ascending again. Rather than shying away from chromatic motion, he embraces it to add tension and a touch of dissonance, particularly in the way he zig-zags up and down the scale. Like all great bass players, he cleverly outlines the harmony of a chord progression, sometimes with chromatic motion or by taking a diatonic approach and adhering to the major or minor scale.

Where Can I Hear Him?
"Crazy Train" Ozzy Osbourne, *Blizzard of Ozz*

It's no surprise that this song is a rock anthem. The grit and attitude of overdriven guitars, the powerful rhythm section, and the eerie, demonic vocals make it a timeless classic. A tutorial in rock bass playing, Daisley manages to fit just about every type of genre-appropriate bass line into this song: punctuated hits, authoritative quarter notes, pedaling, galloping, octave jumps, and scale-based riffs. He clearly defines the harmony of the song, seamlessly transitioning from the minor-based intro, choruses, and solo to the major tonality of the verse. Every bass player should learn how to play this song.

"Sensitive to Light" Rainbow, *Long Live Rock'n'Roll*

There's something undeniably enjoyable about unison rock riffs. Daisley executes the high-energy, blues-scale inspired lines with noticeable ease and brilliant articulation. He pedals the root through the verse and chorus with adrenaline-fueled gusto, adding octave jumps to break up the monotony. Another crash course in rock bass playing, it's difficult not to play air bass while listening to this song.

"Empty Rooms"
Gary Moore, *Live at Isstadion Stockholm*

After the lengthy guitar intro, the band finally kicks in to a sparse, yet perfectly appropriate '80s ballad. Daisley plays with patience, refinement, and restraint to support Moore's vocals. His melodic fretless bass solo puts him in the spotlight, revealing a reserved and incredibly musical player. Using long slides, vibrato, and harmonics, he takes his time and performs with authority.

Bunny Brunel

After discovering the work of legends like Jaco Pastorius and Stanley Clarke, it's only natural for bass players to go through a fusion phase—this is often known as college, or for some, the entirety of one's career. Characterized by exhibitions of higher musical complexity, this style often features the bass in a way that is rarely embraced by popular records and roots genres. Complicated harmony, masterful displays of technical ability, and super funky jams allow aspiring bass players to sharpen their ears, spread their improvisatory wings, and interact with fellow instrumentalists. An exemplary player in this genre is Bunny Brunel, known for his associations with Chick Corea, Mike Stern, Herbie Hancock, Stanley Clarke, and countless others. With his signature basses, educational books and DVDs, and extensive career as a composer and producer, Brunel is most definitely a bass player to know.

Who Is Bunny Brunel?

Brunel grew up in France, where he began playing bass as a teenager. While mostly self-taught, he did attend a music conservatory to focus on upright technique and later ventured into fretless bass. Heavily influenced by jazz and Brazilian music, he spent most of his 20s working with various artists and touring through Europe. While performing in London at Ronnie Scott's, he was introduced to Chick Corea who invited him to come to the United States. Brunel joined Corea's band and recorded the albums *Secret Agent, Tap Step,* and *Summer Jam, 1979: Live Under the Sky.* This quickly solidified him as a force to be reckoned with in the jazz community.

Throughout the 1980s and 1990s, Brunel worked with other artists, including jazz trumpeter Allen Vizzutti and guitarist Kazumi Watanabe. He began stretching out as a composer and producer by releasing solo records such as *Ivanhoe, For You To Play,* and *Momentum.* In the early 2000s, he collaborated with jazz heavyweights Tony MacAlpine, Dennis Chambers, Brian Auger, and others in the CAB project, earning a few Grammy nominations. Between his work with CAB, solo records, and the "Bunny Brunel & Friends" projects featuring players such as Stanley Clarke, Victor Wooten, and Steve Bailey, he continues to be a prominent figure in the musical community.

Let's Talk Style

A technical virtuoso, Brunel continues to carry the torch of boundary-pushing jazz and fusion. His original compositions and collaborations with CAB focus on integrating various forms of right-hand technique, including laid-back fingerstyle playing, rapid-fire sixteenth note grooves, as well as slapping and popping. Brunel adds another layer of rhythmic complexity with a particularly versatile fretting hand. His slap and pop grooves rely heavily on hammer-ons, pull-offs, and open strings. Utilizing the full range of the instrument, his bass lines are intricate, catchy, and creative.

Excelling on upright, electric, and fretless bass, his compositions highlight and explore the sonic possibilities of each instrument. Regularly favoring the fretless, he embraces the unique capabilities of the instrument—harmonics, long slides, and tone—especially when playing Latin or African inspired music. Brunel's compositions and style conjure images of Jaco, Bona, and Clarke, while reflecting his own personality and voice as a superb instrumentalist.

Where Can I Hear Him?
"Bass Ackward" CAB, *CAB 4*
This tune prominently features Brunel's technical mastery with the slapped and hammer-on-heavy opening line. The B-section settles into the pocket with an intensely funky groove with root-octave jumps, up-beat accents, and generous usage of whole and half-step

toggling. An intricate transition gives way to solos where Bunny integrates harmonics, melodic phrases, and blazing ascending patterns.

"Dede" Bunny Brunel, *Ivanhoe*

This high-energy tune embraces the classic, '70s era, Jaco-esque, sixteenth note groove. Accompanied by a slinky rhythm guitar and punchy horn lines, Brunel plays the fretless with an aggressive and staccato approach, accenting the lead lines with quick jumps to the higher register. The slap bass breakdown serves as a stanky bed for the solos before transitioning to the third section featuring a solid groove. Brunel utilizes high harmonics, quick triplet lines, and descending slides that tend to speak well on the fretless.

"Everywhere" Bunny Brunel & Friends, *Café Au Lait*

Showcasing his mellow and melodic side, Brunel transports the listener to a relaxed jazz café. This composition relies on traditional combo instrumentation, with Brunel taking the melody on the fretless bass. He then switches to upright to back the piano and trumpet solos, assuming a solid and supportive role as the trumpet plays the final melody.

Richard Bona

Whenever I think about world music, or the sounds, styles, and instruments of different cultures, I frequently recall records featuring Richard Bona. His playing is beautiful and unique, rooted in African rhythms and infused with jazzy harmonic sensibilities. His unmistakable falsetto vocals and talent as a multi-instrumentalist result in records that are diverse and imaginative, layered with catchy melodies and complex grooves.

Who Is Richard Bona?
A native of Minta, a village in Cameroon, Bona took to music as a child and quickly began playing anything he could get his hands on: guitar, percussion, flute, and more. After moving to Douala at age 11, he started performing around the city with various bands. A local French jazz club encouraged him to put a band together and allowed Bona access to the club owners' record collection. Upon hearing Jaco Pastorius' self-titled album, he became fascinated by the electric bass.

As Bona continued to study, compose, and perform, he spent time in France and Germany, eventually moving to New York. He landed the bass chair in Joe Zawinul's band in the mid-1990s and soon found himself playing alongside countless jazz artists. Since then, he has worked with the Jaco Pastorius Big Band, Harry Belafonte, Randy Brecker, The Pat Metheny Group, Bobby McFerrin, George Benson, Mike Stern, Lee Ritenour, Bela Fleck, and countless others. Bona has also enjoyed success as a solo artist, especially after receiving a Grammy nomination for his 2007 effort, *Tiki*. His technical mastery, superb musicality, and desire to integrate sounds from cultures around the world make each record inspiring and fresh.

Let's Talk Style

Listening to Richard Bona is like visiting a bakery that excels at making every kind of treat. From flaky pastries to indulgent tray bakes, elaborate cakes to finessed tarts, everything is fantastic. You want to try everything they make, because you know the baker has practiced and perfected every recipe. It's easy to say the same thing about Richard Bona. His bass playing, singing, compositional skills, and improvisatory ideas are all at the highest level. He is a remarkably talented individual, who, like the baker, has practiced and developed every aspect of his craft. His solo records are the vast display cases that show off the diversity and range of his musical mind and his bass playing is nothing short of delicious.

It's no wonder that Bona took to the music of Pastorius; his tone, fretless playing, athletic right hand, use of harmonics, and soloing are clearly reminiscent of Jaco's style. He plays with a funky and percussive edge, integrating rhythmic punctuation, dead notes, audible hiccups, and slides. Whether performing on his solo records or working with artists like Mike Stern and Joe Zawinul, Bona places great importance on solid, syncopated, and repetitive rhythmic patterns—no doubt a link to his Cameroonian heritage and experiences traveling the world.

Bona effortlessly shifts among plucking-hand techniques, switching easily from traditional fingerstyle, to slap and pop, to palm muting, to using his thumb, index and middle fingers to play root notes and chords. He takes full advantage of the range of the instrument, often accenting notes with their respective octave, adding high melodies and chords, and returning to the lower notes on the B and E strings. As a soloist, he references vocal melodies, horn parts, and familiar musical quotes while throwing in quick, technique driven lines and clever chord substitutions.

Where Can I Hear Him?

"Please Don't Stop"
Richard Bona and John Legend, *Tiki*
This track speaks to Bona's pop sensibilities with the perfect balance of structure, groove, melody, and harmony. Legend and Bona trade verses in their respective languages, bringing together soulful lyrics from different regions. Marked by some seriously funky licks and a hard-hitting groove, the track shows off Bona's mastery of technique, integrating quick plucking-hand rhythms, slaps, pops, and fingerstyle fills. Multiple listens may be required and desired.

"Shiva Mantra" Richard Bona, *Ten Shades of Blue*
Focused around an Indian-inspired soundscape, this song is layered with intricate harmonies, percussion accents, and unique melodies. As the song progresses, you can hear quick high-register phrases, fretless slides, and a percussive vocal riff mimicked by the bass. This song is a great anchor for the record, embracing Bona's multicultural influences and diverse musical relationships.

"Silver Lining" Mike Stern, *These Times*
Richard Bona has collaborated with Mike Stern on a number of projects as both a bassist and vocalist. Here, he effortlessly lays down a groove, complete with percussive hiccups and quick rhythmic flourishes. He also jumps in with beautiful falsetto vocals,

accented by the guitar melody and the descending diatonic line played in unison at the end of the verse. The song transitions into a fast-paced, funky section marked by a chromatic bass line, building tension until the music opens up, calms down, and sets up the solos. Bona's remarkable right hand drives the song, keeping pace with the rhythmic nuances of the drums and percussion.

Tony Garnier

I'm a firm believer in keeping good company. Entrepreneurs need a solid team, Presidents need a strong cabinet, and songwriters need a great band. After Bob Dylan was awarded the Nobel Prize, I figured it was time to revisit his catalogue to gain insight into the players that bring his music to life. Certainly, someone of his stature will seek out the best of the best, as he did in the 1960s with Rick Danko and The Band. Fast-forward to 1989, when bassist Tony Garnier began as Dylan's bass player and musical director. A particularly soulful upright and electric player, he has toured and recorded with Dylan longer than any other sideman. Having also worked with Asleep At The Wheel, Tom Waits, Loudon Wainwright III, Paul Simon, and many others, he's a master of American roots music and a brilliant interpreter of song form.

Who Is Tony Garnier?
Born in St. Paul, Minnesota, Tony Garnier began playing both upright and electric bass in junior high school. Coming from a long

line of musicians, including his grandfather who led the Camelia Brass Band of New Orleans, he and his siblings took to a variety of instruments and musical styles. After moving to the Bay Area to attend U.C. Berkeley, he began performing live and got a call to join Asleep At The Wheel. A few tours and records later, he ended up in New York to pursue jazz, rock, and rockabilly, landing a gig with Robert Gordon. During the late 1970s and 1980s, he developed his chops as a session musician playing on records by Tom Waits, Buster Poindexter, and Marshall Crenshaw.

In 1989, Garnier was asked to join Bob Dylan on tour in Europe and has maintained the bass position ever since. Featured on most of his records since 1990, including *Time Out Of Mind*, *Love And Theft*, *Modern Times*, and many others, he has also served as Dylan's music director. Known for his impeccable upright playing and "for the song" mentality, he has also recorded with Paul Simon, Iron and Wine, Lucinda Williams, Buddy Guy, Jim Lauderdale, and continues to tour with Dylan.

Let's Talk Style
As listeners, composers, and musicians, our familiarity with what has become known as "The Great American Song Book" serves as insight into the past and inspiration for the future. As bass players, we can listen to Garnier's playing as an authentic approach to the diversity inherent in American folk music. Since the start of his longtime association with Asleep At The Wheel, Garnier has

demonstrated a mastery of old-time country feels, "tic tac" bass, bluegrass, western swing music, jazz, and traditional folk. Comfortable on both upright and electric, he is able to switch back and forth between classical and modern technique in order to best serve the song. He constantly exhibits great tone and intonation whether he's bowing on the upright, walking through changes, or playing a busier electric bass line.

One of Garnier's gifts is his ability to interpret a song in a variety of ways. Bob Dylan is an artist notorious for changing arrangements on a whim, and Garnier is able to adapt and refine his approach to these classic songs wherever his boss takes them. His attention as a listener and player, as well as his encyclopedic knowledge of various styles, makes him the perfect fit for playing with this chameleon-like artist. Garnier's creative and flexible approach also makes him an ideal session musician; whether playing up-tempo rockabilly and blues or melancholy ballads, his extensive knowledge and flawless execution make him an easy first call.

Where Can I Hear Him?
"Sugar Baby" Bob Dylan, *Love And Theft*
Providing a beautifully simple bass line to anchor this song, Garnier acts as both the rhythmic and harmonic foundation of the band. During the verses, he mimics the guitar pattern and integrates gentle arpeggiation to add rhythmic movement on the minor chords. He

takes a smart approach to the octave, jumping from high to low on the upbeats during the bridge. This serves as a welcome departure from the original bass line and highlights his fantastic upright tone.

"Jumpin' At The Woodside"
Asleep At The Wheel, *Asleep At The Wheel*

A diverse sampling of American roots music, this record features Garnier as the backbone of the band, showing off his mastery of traditional country, bluegrass, and big-band inspired swing feels. On this tune he briskly walks through the changes, often doubling the notes on the I chord, walking chromatically from the ii to the V, and adding complexity as solos continue.

"Reason To Cry" Lucina Williams, *Essence*

A heartfelt ballad with a quintessential country feel, Garnier moves gracefully through the changes. While he mostly adheres to the root-3_{rd}-5_{th} approach, he sneaks in occasional chromatic notes and sparse rhythmic fills. His playing is stripped down, complementary, and exactly right.

Edgar Meyer

There's nothing like being in a symphony hall and experiencing the sound of a double bass. The tone of the instrument is enhanced by the beauty of the room and the reverence for hundreds of years of composition. The low, resonant tones fill the space like fresh coffee being poured into your favorite mug; they are rich and comforting, aurally aromatic and sensual. One particular symphony hall concert I attended featured Punch Brothers and their bassist Paul Kowert, a truly exceptional player who will likely have a long and prosperous career. As I looked up from my seat during the intermission, the great Edgar Meyer happened to be chatting with someone a few rows up. Kowert, who studied under Meyer at the Curtis Institute of music, exhibited the musicality, patience, technical precision, and grace of a master—traits that were likely encouraged and nurtured by Meyer. For those unfamiliar with Edgar Meyer, the beauty of his playing is immeasurable, the eclecticism of his musical repertoire unrivaled, and the company he keeps reflective of his brilliance and reputation. A certified genius and an accomplished performer of classical, jazz, bluegrass, and world music, Edgar Meyer is a bass player to know.

Who Is Edgar Meyer?
The son of a bass player and a high school music teacher, Edgar Meyer immediately took to the double bass and began studying at age five. He continued his education at Indiana University and the Aspen Music School under famed double bassist and educator, Stuart Sankey. Throughout the 1980s and early 1990s, he recorded with countless country, bluegrass, and Americana artists, including Garth Brooks, Lyle Lovett, Jerry Douglas, Travis Tritt, and Emmylou Harris. He has been the recipient of numerous awards, including the Avery Fisher Career Grant in 1994, the Avery Fisher Prize in 2000, and the MacArthur Award in 2002.

Celebrated for his varied musical ability, compositional practices, and solo performances, he has performed with Joshua Bell and the St. Paul Chamber Orchestra, The Boston Symphony Orchestra, The Los Angeles Chamber Orchestra, The Nashville Symphony, and many others. A self-titled solo project, released in 2006, featured original compositions and demonstrated his versatility as a multi-instrumentalist. He has collaborated and performed with fellow bassist Christian McBride and has released projects with Yo-Yo Ma, Bela Fleck and Zakir Hussain, and mandolin virtuoso Chris Thile. The 2012 release of *The Goat Rodeo Sessions*, featuring Meyer, Yo-Yo Ma, Thile, and Stuart

Duncan, earned him a Grammy for Best Folk Album. A visiting professor at the Curtis Institute of Music, he continues to compose, record, and perform the world over.

Let's Talk Style

As with all great musicians, their instrument is their voice—a medium of expression so obviously representative of their personality and style it communicates as much or more than words ever could. The double bass is clearly an extension of Edgar Meyer; his playing is a soulful, organic, and amazingly eloquent form of expression. The purity of his tone is something to which every instrumentalist should aspire—the combination of a beautiful instrument and a player perfectly in tune with it. He plays each note deliberately, with keen attention to duration, dynamics, and function. Backed by years of study, he performs and composes in a way that exhibits technical mastery, flawless intonation, and utmost musicality.

It's often said that a person is only as good as the company they keep, and in Meyer's case, that is an esteemed group of the world's greatest musicians. His collaborations are eclectic both in genre and instrumentation, from classical duets with Joshua Bell to bluegrass ensembles with Bela Fleck or Chris Thile. Meyer fits in with the greatest of ease, honoring the traditions of the genre while integrating his own voice.

Meyer often plays in drummerless situations, holding himself and the other musicians fully accountable for rhythm and time keeping. Whether he is playing fingerstyle or bowing, his ability to dictate time is impeccable; his pizzicato notes are quick, even, and precise. He breathes life into bowed notes, enhancing the dynamics of a single note by the way he glides across the strings. He has a diverse take on melody, combining Bach-style arpeggiation with the brisk, modal nature of bluegrass and traditional folk music. Unafraid of the higher register, he has incredible intonation and dexterity in thumb position, taking advantage of the full range of the instrument and harmonics.

Where Can I Hear Him?
"Roundabout" Edgar Meyer, *Edgar Meyer*
The depth of Meyer's musicality is difficult to fathom, especially when you hear his solo record and realize that not only is he a virtuoso bass player, but an extraordinary multi-instrumentalist. This song takes the listener down a fast-paced rabbit hole of bass and piano interplay, only to fall into a soft bed of guitar and long, bowed notes on the double bass. The two sections compete against one another until the conclusion of the song, where the initial piano theme plays over the melancholy chords of the B section. Finally, on a more aggressive bass part fueled by bowing and plucking, he displays his unparalleled mastery of technique.

"Less Is Moi" Yo-Yo Ma, Stuart Duncan, Edgar Meyer, and Chris Thile, *The Goat Rodeo Sessions*

This record showcases a modern string ensemble infused with bluegrass and world music. Meyer and Thile lay the rhythmic foundation on "Less Is Moi" with an up-beat groove, leaving space for Ma to take the melody. Meyer is featured with a beautifully bowed bass solo, where he explores the range of the instrument with soulful low notes followed by climbing melodic lines. As the song progresses, he creeps in with the original bass theme to support the mandolin solo. His groove is undeniably funky but uncluttered, showing the perfect amount of attitude, restraint, and respect for function in the ensemble.

"Concert Duo Mvt 1"
Edgar Meyer and Joshua Bell, *The Best Of Edgar Meyer*

A beautiful duet with an equally brilliant instrumentalist, this features Meyer's talent for melodic counterpoint. A conversational piece, the violin and bass feed on each other dynamically, exhibiting gentle restraint during the contemplative moments and forceful, technically difficult dialogue during moments of heightened emotion. Meyer often jumps positions, especially when he grabs the melody of the piece, and takes advantage of the grand nature of the instrument's lowest notes against the violin. He integrates chords, classical arpeggiation, and chromatic movement throughout the piece, only to conclude with a reinterpretation of the opening theme.

Gail Ann Dorsey

A stellar vocalist and compelling player, Gail Ann Dorsey has had a reputable career as a solo artist and side woman. In addition to being the longtime touring bassist for David Bowie, she has also recorded and toured with Tears for Fears and Lenny Kravitz. With impeccable style, grace, and groove, she is keenly aware of how to support other artists while maintaining the integrity of her own voice.

Who is Gail Ann Dorsey?
Gain Ann Dorsey was born and bred in Philadelphia, a city with quite the reputation for birthing funky bass players. At first favoring guitar, Dorsey acquired a bass when she was 14 but took it up with greater ambition in her early 20s. Harboring a passion for writing and producing films, she attended the California Institute of the Arts for Live Action Film, but the notorious uncertainty of the film industry inspired her to turn to a career in music. Upon moving to London at the age of 22, Dorsey began collaborating with a number

of artists and eventually landed a record deal with Warner Music Group. She released her first solo record, *The Corporate World*, in 1988 with the help of producer and fellow bass player, Nathan East. While establishing herself in the London music scene, she switched to Island Records and released her second solo effort, *Rude Blue*.

By the mid-1990s, Dorsey began to focus on session work and collaborating with other artists, including Gang of Four and Tears for Fears. In 1995, she joined David Bowie's band, where she provided stunning vocals and bass lines on subsequent tours and records. Other artists she has recorded and toured with include the Indigo Girls, Dar Williams, Joan Osborne, Suzanne Vega, Gwen Stefani, and Boy George. Dorsey continues to play an active role as both a bass player and vocalist, and released her third solo record, *I Used To Be...*, in 2004.

Let's Talk Style

After years of listening to music, you begin to distinguish the sound and personality of certain bass players. Dorsey, typically sporting a powerful and mid-range prominent Music Man instrument, is always heard loud and clear.

Although her playing is steeped in soul and R&B, Gail tends to steer away from typical dead notes in favor of a concise groove and clean attack. She places emphasis on each individual note, thereby creating a deep and distinctive pocket. With plenty of experience playing pop and rock music, she is very much aware of how to enhance and drive a song, whether it's with pulsing eighth notes or a composed part. Some of her more notable bass lines are derived from the minor-pentatonic scale, relying on a solid rhythmic framework and the root, 5_{th}, and $b7_{th}$.

One of Dorsey's greatest attributes as a player comes from her knowledge of melody, phrasing, and space. During moments of elongated vocal notes, she strings together elegant melodic bass lines that take advantage of the air within the music. This lifts the song to greater heights, adding beauty and strength to already powerful lyrical phrases. Her melody lines are clean and graceful, played with an air of confidence and a knack for voice leading.

Where Can I Hear Her?

"Under Pressure" David Bowie, *A Reality Tour*

With her signature tone, piercing vocals, and precise execution of one of the most celebrated bass lines in popular music, it's obvious why Gail became a mainstay in Bowie's band. She takes a dignified approach to playing the song by remaining true to the recorded bass line and shines as a vocalist when sharing the lead duties with Bowie.

"Falling Down" Tears For Fears, *Raoul And The Kings Of Spain*

Dorsey flexes her rock muscles with a minor pentatonic-themed line during the verses, a heavy and funky approach to the choruses, and a syncopated climbing line à la "I Feel Good" before ushering in the next verse. As she returns to the initial groove, she again provides the groundwork for the band's signature lofty vocals and atmospheric guitar work. As the song progresses, she plays with register, adding higher embellishments to the initial groove and sneaking in fills throughout the final chorus.

"Magical" Gail Ann Dorsey, *I Used To Be...*

A great example of her clear and confident playing style, Dorsey settles into a simple yet funky groove during the verses. Playing to the chords, she supports the song with clean root notes, rhythmic fills, and elegant counter melodies that support long vocal notes. The song breaks down into an ascending melodic line and a concise, lovely solo before transitioning back to the verse and chorus.

Chris Wood

A master of both the upright and electric bass, Chris Wood exhibits superior technical skill, boundless imagination, and reverence for traditional and modern styles. Best known for his work with The Wood Brothers and Medeski, Martin and Wood, his recording credits and hard-working attitude represent continual artistic growth.

Who Is Chris Wood?
Chris Wood spent his childhood in Colorado with parents who enjoyed music and poetry, inspiring their children to do the same. Strongly influenced by folk, blues, and jazz, his musical journey led him to leave Colorado and attend the New England Conservatory in Boston. At school, he focused on ensemble playing and studied with jazz greats Dave Holland, John McNeil, George Garzone, Bob Moses, and Geri Allen. While living in Boston, Bob Moses introduced Chris to John Medeski at a session and the players bonded immediately.

After discovering their musical connection, Medeski and Wood moved to New York, picking up jazz gigs at the Village Gate, and forming a trio with drummer Billy Martin. The band released their first album in 1992 and quickly attracted forward-thinking listeners with experimental song forms and improvisatory live performances.

While Chris Wood remained busy with MM&W, he also shared the stage with his brother, Oliver, who had been touring and playing with the group King Johnson. The brothers soon began writing together and signed to Blue Note in 2006, releasing their first record, *Ways Not To Lose*. Many years and record deals later, they received a Grammy nomination for their 2018 album, *One Drop Of Truth*. With a busy touring schedule and the endless desire to create, The Wood Brothers continue to evolve by making records that explore traditional roots music, clever songwriting, and musicality at the highest level.

While not on the road, Chris Wood is often called upon as a session player. His versatility as a bassist and vocalist has landed him credits with Mike Stern, Natalie Merchant, Marc Ribot, Seth Walker, and Amy Ray of the Indigo Girls.

Let's Talk Style

Whether you're listening to the avant-garde stylings of Medeski, Martin & Wood or the simpler, soulful tunes of The Wood Brothers, Chris' bass playing is nothing short of remarkable. He's been lucky enough to participate in projects that feature him as an artist, rather than a sideman or behind the scenes player. Coupled with the fact that he composes much of the music, he's got plenty of room to experiment, develop, and showcase his talents.

The music made by Medeski, Martin & Wood as a trio and in collaboration with John Scofield, combines elements of jazz, funk, and soul with inventive song form and unrestrained improvisation. Known for free-form jams, each player is given room to experiment with sound, technique, and style. As the themes evolve, the players give each other room to stretch, encouraging experimentation and long-form soloing. Wood embraces this freedom and often goes back and forth between different techniques—bowing, pizzicato fingerstyle, ringing open strings, long slides up and down the neck, muted or "dub" style grooves, chords, harmonics, and noise. He's also known for implementing the "bass snare" sound, created by placing paper below the strings so that the attack has a percussive snap.

Playing with The Wood Brothers, Chris takes a more traditional approach to song form due to the nature of the genre. Switching between upright and electric, he continues to compose sophisticated bass lines that anchor the song, evolve dynamically, and allow for live improvisation. His musical contributions as a songwriter, vocalist, and harmonica player enhance the overall sound of the trio, resulting in a band that sounds far larger than you would expect.

Where Can I Hear Him?

"Rise Up" Medeski, Martin & Wood, *Tonic*

This live version of "Rise Up" kicks off with a short piano intro before Wood's uber funky groove takes over, making you feel like you're walking around the bustling streets of the New York City's West Village. Breaking down into a solo piano section reminiscent of Southern gospel music, the song transitions back into high-energy jazz land. Medeski and Martin then fade out, leaving space for Wood to play a free-form solo with plenty of space, intriguing dissonance, and exciting technical runs.

"Keep Me Around" The Wood Brothers, *The Muse*

This composition by The Wood Brothers features Wood on acoustic bass performing an organic and extraordinarily funky groove that wouldn't be the same on an electric. He sets the tone of the song with a perfectly composed part that evokes Lou Reed's "Take A Walk On The Wild Side" due to the I-IV chord progression. Beginning on the root, he plays a brisk chromatic line to accent the 3_{rd} of the chord, descends by way of raking the open strings, and plays an ascending slide into the IV chord. He switches to a classic root-5_{th} part for the pre-chorus before reintroducing the groove during the hook of the song.

"Wastin' My Mind"
The Wood Brothers, *Live At The Barn*

Chris kicks this off with a dirty, overdriven bass tone and a gritty groove to match. As the introduction develops rhythmically and gives way to tight vocal harmonies, the band showcases their greatest asset: complex and complimentary sounds that fit together like a glove. During the guitar solo and breakdown, Chris and Oliver have a brief conversation, punctuated by high-register chords, punchy single notes, and a hard-hitting groove to build dynamics before the soaring vocal harmonies of the chorus.

Justin Meldal-Johnsen

As a teenager, the thrill of seeing your favorite band live for the first time is tremendously exciting. You've waited for months, anticipating the night when you finally get to go to the first concert *you* chose to go to—that your parents allowed. As someone who spent a good portion of middle school listening to the retro-soul feels and modern experimental sounds contained on *Odelay* and *Mutations,* I couldn't wait for my first "grown up" concert experience: Beck on the *Midnight Vultures* tour. The show was incredible and I walked away feeling I had witnessed something truly special. It was Justin Meldal-Johnsen holding down the low end, acting as both bass player and musical director. Little did I know that would barely scratch the surface of his talent and career achievements.

Who Is Justin Meldal-Johnsen?
Justin Meldal-Johnsen's family stereo featured all kinds of music and he instinctively gravitated towards the bass. An L.A. native, he

was able to mingle with artists around the local scene and was eager to work in recording studios. After high school, he landed a job as a night-shift janitor at Cherokee Studios, where composer and arranger David Campbell frequently worked. Meldal-Johnsen became friends with Cambell's son, Beck, and they began playing music together. By 1996, Meldal-Johnson joined Beck in the studio for *Odelay* and has since served as his longtime bass player and musical director.

As his session player reputation grew, he laid down bass lines for artists like Nelly Furtado, The Dixie Chicks, Pink, Garbage, They Might Be Giants, Sara Bareilles, Ima Robot, Jason Mraz, and countless others. Still a mainstay in Beck's band, he toured with Nine Inch Nails from 2008-2009 and continued to gain notoriety as a writer and producer in L.A. Often called upon for his talent in the world of pop and rock, he has produced records for Macy Gray, Paramore, Neon Trees, M83, Tegan and Sara, Young The Giant, and many others. In 2017, Fender began production of the Justin Meldal-Johnsen Road Worn Mustang, a signature bass modeled after his personal 1966 Mustang.

Let's Talk Style
Justin Meldal-Johnsen is a jack-of-all-trades and master of many. While some players have a clearly identifiable tonal fingerprint, he is completely adaptable. He has a keen ear when it comes to tone, allowing the song and production to dictate the instrument of

choice. Photographed with everything from a Fender Precision, Jazz, or Jaguar to a hollow body Gibson Thunderbird or Upright, he can mimic or create just about any sound. Using a vast array of pedals, synths, and effects, his potential for sonic exploration is unlimited and frequently exercised. With a deep understanding of the tools at hand, his knowledge of gear is an asset that has become particularly useful as a session player and producer.

When it comes to playing, his ability to switch between techniques such as fingerstyle, palm muting, picking, or slapping, is just another element of his musical versatility. His harmonic and stylistic vocabulary is as diverse and developed as his arsenal of instruments. He has the drive and aggression to fit into heavy rock, the innate soulfulness to groove in an R&B context, and the patience and sophistication to support singer-songwriters. While he seems at home in almost any environment, he truly shines in funk-driven pop and rock, where he toggles between catchy lines, driving root notes, and intricate fills.

Where Can I Hear Him?
"Sexx Laws" Beck, *Midnight Vultures*
Meldal-Johnsen brings both rhythmic and harmonic complexity to this track, pushing it along with syncopated root notes and quick dominant-7_{th} inspired fills. He favors the up-beats and provides a funky walk between the chord changes of the chorus, fitting perfectly into the percussive nature of this pop creation. The bass

line is energetic, technically exciting, and complementary to the theme and melody.

"Ain't It Fun" Paramore, *Paramore*
While the bass credit on this track actually goes to Paramore's bass player (Jeremy Davis), Justin Meldal-Johnsen produced the record and helped it land the 2014 Grammy Award for Best Rock Song. His production style with this project is super-charged; it captures the energy of the band with a driving, yet syncopated rhythm section, in-your-face vocals, dynamic breakdowns, thick choir chants, and brilliant synthesizer sounds. The track shows off the best the band has to offer, framing the insightful lyrics with clever marimba-like hooks, overdriven guitars, and an intense groove.

"Dynomite" Ima Robot, *Ima Robot*
Ima Robot reflects founding member Justin Meldal-Johnsen's inner punk rocker. His overdriven tone, fierce picking, and simple part are ideal and respectful to the genre. The evenness of his attack combined with the saturation of his tone demonstrates mastery of both technique and sonic shaping.

Index

A
Adderley, Cannonball, 8
Adler, Lou, 101
Aerosmith, 55-59
Alexander, Arthur, 26
Alpert, Herb, 110
Allen, Geri, 164
Allison, Mose, 42
Allman, Gregg, 97
American Sound Studios, 25
Amos, Tori, 34
Andersen, Eric, 51, 53
Angelico, Ellen, ii
Armstrong, Billie Joe, 78
Armstrong, Kyshona, ii
Armstrong, Louis, 96
Asleep At The Wheel, 150-153
Association, The, 102
Atlantic Records, 25
Auger, Brian, 142

B
Babbitt, Bob, 12-15
Bailey, Steve, 142
Baker, Ginger, 41
Ballard, Frankie, 125
Band, The, 50-54, 150
Band Perry, The, 120
Bareilles, Sara, 170
Beck, 169-171
Beckett, Barry, 21
Belafonte, Harry, 146
Bell, Joshua, 155, 158
Berry, Chuck, 20
Bennett, Tony, 92
Benson, George, 110, 146
Bernstein, Leonard, 132
Big Apple Band, 105
Big Three Trio, 2
Black Sabbath, 137
Blackmore, Ritchie, 137
Blain, Hal, 101
Blues Brothers, The, 17-19, 114
Boston Symphony Orchestra, 155
Bona, Richard, 145-149
Bonamassa, Joe, 120-122
Bond, Graham, 42
Booker T. and the MG's, 16
Boulez, Pierre, 132
Bowie, David, 104, 106, 115, 160-162
Box Tops, The, 26
Boy George, 161
Brecker, Randy, 146
Bridie, Leanne, i
Brooks, Garth, 155
Brothers Johnson, The, 109-113
Brown, Corey, i
Brown, Ray, 91-95, 115
Bruce, Jack, viii, 41-45, 75
Brunel, Bunny, 141-144
Buble, Michael, 125
Buffett, Jimmy, 26, 115
Burrell, Kenny, 8, 132

Burton, Cliff, 63-67
Butler, Geezer, 64
Byrne, David, 34, 68-69

C

Caillat, Colbie, 125
Cale, J.J., 26, 101
Callender, Red, 96-99
Camelia Brass Band, 151
Campbell, David, 170
Campbell, Glen, 100
Capitols, The, 12
Carlton, Larry, 120
Carter, Clarence, 21
Carter, Ron, 115
Carey, Mariah, 72
Carpenters, The, 100, 103
Cash, Rosanne, 115, 120
Caston, Leonard, 2
Chambers, Dennis, 142
Chambers, Paul, viii, 7-11
Chapman, Tony, 46
Charles, Ray, 20
Cher, 21
Chesney, Kenny, 120
Chess Records, 2
Chic, 104-107
Chicken Shack, 136
Chrisman, Gene, 25
Clapton, Eric, 17, 41, 114-115
Clarke, Stanley, 63, 110, 141, 142
Clash, The, 59-61
Clay, Otis, 30
Cobain, Kurt, 74
Cocker, Joe, 51, 106
Cohen, Leonard, 125
Cole, Nat King, 97
Cooder, Ry, 96
Cooke, Sam, 96
Corea, Chick, 141
Cream, 2, 41-45
Crenshaw, Marshall, 151
Cropper, Steve, 16
Crosby, Bing, 97
Cray, Robert, 30

Coffey, Dennis, 15
Cogbill, Tommy, 25-28
Coltrane, John, 8

D

Daisley, Bob, 136-140
Danko, Rick, 50-54, 150
Davis, Miles, 8-11, 132
Davis, Richard, 131-135
DeJohnette, Jack, 114
Diamond, Neil, 26, 101
Diddley, Bo, 114
Dio, Ronnie James, 137
Dirnt, Mike, 75, 78-82
Dixie Chicks, The, 170
Dixon, Willie, 1-6, 7, 17
Dolphy, Eric, 132
Doobie Brothers, The, 115-117
Dorsey, Gail Ann, 160-163
Dorsey, Lee, 34
Douglas, Jerry, 155
Dr. John, 34
Duncan, Stuart, 155, 158
Dunn, Duck, 16-19, 26
Duran Duran, 106
Dyett, Walter, 131
Dylan, Bob, 17, 50-54, 60, 150-152

E

East, Nathan, 161
Edwards, Bernard, 104-108
Ellington, Duke, 92, 95
Emmons, Bobby, 25
Eno, Brian, 68-69
Etheridge, Melissa, 30, 125
Evans, Bill, 10
Evans, Don, ii
Evans, Gil, 8
Eyes Adrift, 74

F

FAME Studios, 21, 25
Fender, Leo, 110
Fitzgerald, Ella, 91-92
Five Breezes, The, 2
Fjeld, Jonas, 51, 53

Fleck, Bela, 146, 155-156
Flipper, 74
Floyd, Eddie, 16, 21
Fortunate Sons, The, 120
Four Jumps of Jive, The, 2
Foxboro Hot Tubs, 79
Franklin, Aretha, 21, 26, 28, 110
Francis, Benjamin "Poppi," 33
Frantz, Chris, 69
Frustrators, The, 79, 81
Funk Brothers, The, 13
Furtado, Nelly, 170

G

Gamble and Huff, 13
Gang of Four, 161
Garbage, 170
Garland, Red, 8
Garnier, Tony, 150-153
Garner, Erroll, 97
Garzone, George, 164
Gaye, Marvin, 13
Germantown Dots, The, 29
Getz, Stan, 132
Giants In The Trees, 75
Gill, Vince, 115, 120, 122
Gillespie, Dizzy, 91
Golden World Studios, 12
Gordon, Robert, 151
Gorillaz, 60-62, 69
Green Day, 78-81
Groban, Josh, 125
Grohl, Dave, 74
Graham, Larry, 7, 110
Grant, Amy, 101
Gray, Macy, 170
Green, Al, 29-31
Green, Benny, 8
Greenwood, Colin, 83-86
Greenwood, Johnny, 84
Guthrie, Arlo, 125
Guy, Buddy, 115, 151

H

Haggard, Merle, 101
Hall, Rick, 20
Haller, Craig, i
Hamilton, Tom, 55-58
Hancock, Herbie, 110, 141
Hanrahan, Kip, 42
Happy Mondays, 69
Harris, Emmylou, 51, 155
Harrison, George, 115
Hathaway, Donny, 115-116
Havana 3am, 60
Hawkins, Roger, 21
Hawkins, Ronnie, 50
Hayes, Isaac, 16, 114
Haynes, Warren, 33
Helm, Levon, 21, 50-53
Hetfield, James, 64
Hi Rhythm Section, 29-32
Hill, Faith, 120
Hines, Earl, 97
Hitsville, Studio A, 12
Hodges, Charles, 29
Hodges, Leroy, 29-32
Hodges, Teenie, 29
Holiday, Billie, 96-97
Holland, Dave, 164
Hood, David, 20-24, 26
Hughes, Sean, 79
Hurley, Sean, 124-127
Hussain, Zakir, 155

I

Ian, Janis, 131-135
Ima Robot, 170, 172
Impalas, The, 29
Indigo Girls, 161, 165
Iron and Wine, 151

J

Jackson, Al Jr., 16, 29
Jackson, Michael, 109, 112
Jagger, Mick, 47, 106
Jam Band, The, 56
Jamerson, James, v, 13, 17, 26, 32, 115-16

James, Etta, 21, 115,
Joel, Billy, 101
Johnson, J.J., 8
Johnson, Jimmy, 21
Johnson, Kevin, i
Johnson, Louis, 109-113
Jones, Booker T., 16, 29
Jones, Elvin, 132, 134
Jones, Mick, 60
Jones, Philly Joe, 8
Jones, Quincy, 91-92, 109-112
Jones, Rickie Lee, 97, 99
Joyride, 34
Judd, Wynonna, 115

K
Kahvas Jute, 136
Keith, Toby, 120
Kelly, Wynton, 8, 11
Keys, Alicia, 125
Kiffmeyer, John, 78
King, Albert, 16, 19, 34
King, B.B., 114
King, Freddie, 16
King Johnson, 165
Knechtel, Larry, 101
Korner, Alexis, 42
Kowert, Paul, 154
Kravitz, Lenny, 160
Knight, Gladys, 13-14
Kristofferson, Kris, 26

L
LaBelle, Patti, 34
Lady Antebellum, 120
Lauderdale, Jim, 151
Led Zeppelin, 2
Lee, Geddy, 64, 75
Legend, John, 148
Lemmy, 75
Lennox, Annie, 125, 127
Lewis, Jerry Lee, 16
Los Angeles Chamber Orchestra, 155
Lovett, Lyle, 155
Lynott, Phil, 63

Lynyrd Skynyrd, 21

M
M83, 170
Ma, Yo-Yo, 155, 158
MacAlpine, Tony, 142
Madonna, 104, 106, 108
Mahal, Taj, 34
Makowksi, Chet, ii
Malmsteen, Yngwie, 137
Mamas and The Papas, The, 100
Mann, Manfred, 42
Martin, Billy, 165
Martino, Pat, 132
Mayall, John, 42
Mayer, John, 115, 125, 127
McBride, Christian, 155
McCartney, Paul, 7, 75
McDonald, Michael, 109, 110, 115
McEntire, Reba, 120
McLean, Jackie, 8
McFerrin, Bobby, 146
McNeil, John, 164
Medeski, John, 164-167
Meldal-Johnson, Justin, 169-172
Mellencamp, John, 115
Memphis Horns, The, 29
Menzel, Idina, 125
Merchant, Natalie, 165
Meters, The, 33-36
Metallica, 63-67
Metheny, Pat, 146
Meyer, Edgar, 154-159
Michilli, Alicia, ii
Mingus, Charles, 97
Mitchell, Willie, 29
Mo', Keb', 115
Modeliste, Zigaboo, 33-35
Modern Jazz Quartet, 92
Moman, Chips, 25
Monkees, The, 96, 101
Montgomery, Wes, 8, 11, 132
Moore, Gary, 137-140
Morgan, Lee, 8
Morrison, Van, 131-135
Morrissette, Alanis, 125

Moses, Bob, 164
Mraz, Jason, 170
Mungo Jerry, 136
Muscle Shoals, 20-25
Mystics, The, 20

N
Nashville Symphony, 155
Nelson, Ricky, 100-101
Neon Trees, 170
Neville, Aaron, 33, 120
Newman, Randy, 97, 115
Nine Inch Nails, 170
Nirvana, iii, 73-77
No WTO Combo, The, 74
Nocentelli, Leo, 34
Notorious B.I.G., 105
Novoselic, Krist, iii, 73-77
Nyro, Laura, 21, 132

O
O'Brien, Ed, 84
Offspring, The, 78
On A Friday, 84
Osborn, Joe, 100-103
Osborne, Joan, 120, 161
Osbourne, Ozzy, 136-139

P
Palmer, Robert, 34, 37, 104, 106
Paramore, 170, 172
Parker, Charlie, 91, 96
Partridge Family, The, 101
Pastorius, Jaco, v, 141, 145-147
Peebles, Ann, 29-32
Perry, Joe, 55
Peterson, Oscar, 91-94
Petty, Tom, 17
Pickett, Wilson, 16, 21, 26
Pink, 170
Philadelphia International, 13
Phillips, Derrek, ii
Players, The, 120
Poindexter, Buster, 151
Porter, Jr., George, 33-37

Power Station, The, 106
Presley, Elvis, 16, 26
Preston, Billy, 109, 114
Prine, John, 16
Pritchard, Michael Ryan, 78
Punch Brothers, 154

Q
Quinichette, Paul, 8

R
Radiohead, 83-86
Rainbow, 136, 139
Rainey, Chuck, 119
Ray, Amy, 165
Redding, Noel, 75
Redding, Otis, 16, 18
Reed, Jimmy, 20
Reed, Lou, 43, 167
Ribot, Marc, 165
Rich, Alan, 120
Richards, Keith, 47
Ritenour, Lee, 110, 146
Rivers, Johnny, 100
Rhodes, Michael, 119-123
Robertson, Robbie, 34, 50
Rodgers, Nile, 104-107
Rogers, Kenny, 101
Rolling Stones, The, 1, 2, 34, 46-48, 115
Rollins, Sonny, 8
Ronson, Mark, 115
Ross, Diana, 104-105
Ross, Michael, i
Royal Studios, 29-30
Rucker, Darius, 120
Runnin Pardners, The, 34
Russell, Leon, 21

S
Salt-N-Pepa, 105
Sam and Dave, 16
Sankey, Stuart, 155
Scaggs, Boz, 115

Screeching Weasel, 79
Scofield, John, 34, 117, 166
Seger, Bob, 21, 26
Selway, Phil, 84
Silverstone, Alicia, 55
Simon, Paul, 21-23, 106, 131-132, 150-151
Simonon, Paul, 59-62
Sinatra, Frank, 92, 132
Sister Sledge, 104-105
Skaggs, Ricky, 101
Sklar, Leland, 98, 119
Sledge, Percy, 21, 23
Smith, Will, 105
Springfield, Dusty, 26-27
Spinners, The, 15
Springsteen, Bruce, 132
Squirtgun, 79
St. Paul Chamber Orchestra, 155
Staple Singers, The, 16, 22
Stax, 16, 18, 29, 30
Starr, Edwin, 12
Starr, Ringo, 42, 51, 125
Stefani, Gwen, 161
Stern, Mike, 141, 146-149, 165
Stewart, Rod, 105-106, 115
Sting, 75
Straisand, Barbara, 132
Stravinsky, Igor, 132
Striking Matches, 121
Sugarhill Gang, The, 105, 107
Supremes, The, 109
Swampers, The, 21, 24
Sweet Children, 78
Szell, George, 132

T

Talking Heads, 68-71
Tatum, Art, 96-98
Taylor, Andy, 106
Taylor, James, 96, 115
Taylor, Johnnie, 21
Taylor, Koko, 114
Tears For Fears, 160-163
Tegan and Sara, 170
Temptations, The, 13

The 5th Dimension, 100
The Good, The Bad and The Queen, 60, 62
They Might Be Giants, 170
Thicke, Robin, 125
Thile, Chris, 155-158
Thompson, Tony, 106
Tom Tom Club, 68-72
Toussaint, Allen, 34
Traffic, 21, 24
Trauma, 64
Tre Cool, 79
Tritt, Travis, 114, 155
Trower, Robin, 42
Tucker, Tanya, 101
Tyler, Steven, 55

U

Ulrich, Lars, 64, 66
Uriah Heep, 137

V

Van Zandt, Townes, 26, 28
Vaughan, Jimmie, 114
Vaughan, Sarah, 92, 132
Veasley, Gerald, ii
Vega, Suzanne, 161
Vertical Horizon, 124-126
Vizzutti, Allen, 142

W

Wainwright III, Loudon, 150
Waits, Tom, 150-151
Walker, Seth, 165
Washington, Jr., Grover, 110, 114
Watanabe, Kazumi, 142
Waters, Muddy, 2
Watts, Charlie, 46-47
Walter, Little, 2
Wasner, Casey, ii
Wayne's World, 56
Weeks, Willie, 96, 99, 114-118
Weezer, 78
Wexler, Jerry, 25
Weymouth, Tina, 68-72
Widowmaker, 136

Williams, Dar, 161
Williams, Jr., Hank, 120
Williams, Lucinda, 151, 153
Wilson, Nancy, 92
Winwood, Steve, 114-115
Withers, Bill, 110
Wolf, Howlin', 2
Womack, Bobby, 109
Wonder, Stevie, 12, 115
Wood Brothers, The, 164-168
Wood, Chris, 164-168
Wood, Oliver, 164-168
Wood, Ron, 115
Wooten, Victor, 142
World Famous Headliners, The, 120
Wrecking Crew, The, 100
Wright, Greg, ii
Wyman, Bill, 46-49

Y
Yorke, Thom, 83
Young, Neil, 51
Young, Reggie, 25
Young The Giant, 170

Z
Zappa, Frank, 42
Zawinul, Joe, 132, 146, 147

Suggested Listening

A
Aerosmith, *Get A Grip*
Aerosmith, *Toys In The Attic*
Albert King, *Born Under A Bad Sign*
Al Green, *Let's Stay Together*
Annie Lennox, *Songs of Mass Destruction*
Ann Peebles, *I Can't Stand The Rain*
Aretha Franklin, *I Never Loved A Man The Way I Love You*
Asleep At The Wheel, *Asleep At The Wheel*

B
The Band, *The Last Waltz*
Beck, *Midnight Vultures*
Bernard Edwards, *Glad To Be Here*
Bill Wyman, *Monkey Grip*
Bill Wyman's Rhythm Kings, *Double Bill, Vol. 1*
The Blues Brothers Band, *The Blues Brothers*
Bob Dylan, *Before The Flood*
Bob Dylan, *Love and Theft*
The Brothers Johnson, *Light Up The Night*
The Brothers Johnson, *Right On Time*

C
CAB, *CAB 4*
Chic, *Rhino Hi-Five: Chic*

The Clash, *London Calling*
Cream, *Goodbye*
Cream, *Royal Albert Hall London May 2-3-5-6 2005*

D
David Bowie, *A Reality Tour*
Dennis Coffey and the Detroit Guitar Band, *Evolution*
The Doobie Brothers, *Farewell Tour*
Donny Hathaway, *Live*
Duke Ellington, Ray Brow, *This One's For Blanton*
Dusty Springfield, *Dusty In Memphis*

E
Edgar Meyer, *Edgar Meyer*
Edger Meyer, Joshua Bell, *The Best of Edgar Meyer*
Elvin Jones, Richard Davis, *Heavy Sounds*

G
Gail Ann Dorsey, *I Used To Be*
Gladys Knight and The Pips, *Imagination*
The Good, The Bad & The Queen, *The Good, The Bad & The Queen*
Gorillaz, Paul Simonon, *Plastic Beach*
Green Day, *21st Century Breakdown*
Green Day, *Dookie*

H
Hi Rhythm Band, *On The Loose*

I
Ima Robot, *Ima Robot*

J
Jack Bruce, *Songs For A Tailor*
Janis Ian, *Between The Lines*
Joe Bonamassa, *Muddy Wolf At Red Rocks (Live)*
John Mayer, *Paradise Valley*

John Scofield, *That's What I Say*

L
Lucina Williams, *Essence*

M
Madonna, *Like A Virgin*
Medeski, Martin, & Wood, *Tonic*
Metallica, *Master of Puppets*
Metallica, *Ride The Lightning*
The Meters, *Rejuvenation*
Michael Jackson, *Off the Wall*
Mike Stern, *These Times*
Miles Davis, *Kind Of Blue*

N
Nirvana, *From The Muddy Banks Of The Wishkah*
Nirvana, *Nevermind*
Nirvana, *Nirvana*

O
Oscar Peterson Trio, *Night Train*
Otis Redding, *Dock Of The Bay*
Ozzy Osbourne, *Blizzard of Ozz*

P
Paramore, Paramore
Paul Chambers, *Bass On Top*
Paul Simon, *Still Crazy After All These Years*
Percy Sledge, *The Best of Percy Sledge*

R
Radiohead, In Rainbows
Radiohead, *OK Computer*
Rainbow, *Long Live Rock 'n' Roll*
Richard Bona, *Ten Shades of Blue*
Richard Bona, *Tiki*

Rick Danko, Jonas Fjeld, Eric Andersen, *One More Shot*
Rickie Lee Jones, *Rickie Lee Jones*
Robert Palmer, *Sneakin' Sally Through The Alley*
The Rolling Stones, *Let It Bleed*

S
The Spinners, *Happiness Is Being With The Spinners*
Striking Matches, *Nothing But The Silence*
Stuart Duncan, Chris Thile, Edgar Meyer, Yo-Yo Ma, *The Goat Rodeo Sessions*

T
Talking Heads, *Talking Heads 77*
Tears For Fears, *Raoul and The Kings of Spain*
Townes Van Zandt, *Flyin' Shoes*
Traffic, *On The Road*

V
Van Morrison, *Astral Weeks*
Vertical Horizon, *Everything You Want*
Vince Gill, *These Days*

W
Willie Dixon, *I Am The Blues*
Willie Dixon, *Poet Of The Blues*
The Wood Brothers, *Live at the Barn*
The Wood Brothers, *The Muse*

About The Author

Ryan Madora is a Nashville-based writer, educator, and bass player. A native of Philadelphia and graduate of New York University, she has been a writer for the online bass publication *No Treble* since 2011. Her touring credits include guitar virtuoso Robben Ford and country music icon Bobby Bones. In addition to backing up artists like Hanson, Carrie Underwood, and Garth Brooks, she has made appearances on the hit TV show, "Nashville." Bringing eclecticism, groove, and musical intention to every gig, she is frequently called upon in the studio and has produced records for her instrumental trio, The Interludes. An educator at heart, she teaches clinics, private lessons, and serves as a faculty member at Musician's Institute Guitar Craft Academy. In her free time, she tends to her garden, expands her culinary repertoire, and takes epic walks with her husband.

Made in the USA
Monee, IL
15 January 2020